Paul and I Discover America

By the same author
Hooked on Books
The Naked Children

Paul and I Discover America

Daniel Fader

GROSSET & DUNLAP
Publishers • New York

For Martha and Lisa

Contents

Violence...

Even for Menlo Park, which has one of the most desirable climates in America, the spring of '58 was unusually fine. One consequence of long companionable evenings for residents of Perry Lane was that several marriages and living arrangements companionably rearranged themselves. Major changes in private lives were reflected in minor alterations within the two-person teams on which our evening frisbee competition was built. Another consequence was that our lane became an evening attraction to neighboring folk who otherwise spent their days and nights hidden among oak and eucalyptus which gave the area the appearance of a forest from above. The number of spectators grew as light waned, talk often became serious as frisbees fell from evening skies, and a single subject came to dominate our darkening conversations. Improbably, in the peace which accompanies exercise followed by liquid replenishment, we spoke of atomic war.

As I write now, fifteen years after those nights of plastic saucers and atomic fears, I have before me a list of materials packed into two cardboard cartons and a polyethylene one-loaf bread box that were permanently stored in the trunk of our car. If I doubt the reality of those fears I have only to read the list, especially its title: SURVIVAL KIT. When the bombs fell on northern California, with its great air bases and manufactories for electronic war, we planned to be among the survivors.

Our breadbox contained a Smith and Wesson .38 special with two-inch barrel, Lawrence holster, and one hundred cartridges with two-hundred-grain lead bullets for stopping power; two leather-handled sheath knives with sharpening stones attached; a Leupold compass with a protected face, and a waterproof matchbox full of wooden matches; a complete first-aid kit, first-aid book, and halazone tablets for water purification; fifty fishhooks in a small Ewing rotary box; a hundred yards of ten-pound monofilament together with bobbins, fish stringer, and assorted splitshot; an Acme Thunderer whistle; a small, fold-ing, plastic magnifying glass; and an official Boy Scout flint and steel with tinder.

In the two cardboard cartons we had packed a lightweight ax, pot, and frying pan, warm clothes, one hundred feet of 7/16-inch nylon climbing rope, two sleeping bags, a transistor radio with extra batteries, two full canteens, two flashlights with extra batteries, forty one-dollar bills and ten dollars worth of nickels, a radiation counter, and fifty dollars worth of canned goods. The three boxes had taken us six months to fill, six monthly expenditures of approximately fifty dollars from an income that never exceeded two hundred dollars a month during that time. Three hundred dollars of carefully purchased protection against atomic war; hummingbirds in the live oak outside our cottage window; long evenings of frisbee and home brew—we had come back to America. The air was full of birdsong and the threat of war.

Our return to America had begun in the very small English village of Hardwick, half an hour's bicycle ride from the university town of Cambridge. Having lived and studied in the town itself for a year and a half, we had moved to the village when our GI Bill ran out and we were offered a rent-free home for spring term. Because of his property, his position in the university, and especially because of his person, the owner of the house was squire of the village. Because my wife and I were living in his house, looking after his property and his children, I found I had inherited some part of his authority together with his seat in the village pub.

To have men of the village tip their caps and women bow their heads in respectful greeting was unsettling enough. More difficult were the occasional requests to arbitrate disputes about which I had little information and less understanding of the angry dialect. Worst of all was the universal expectation that I could speak for my country. As the first American many villagers had spoken with since the war, my presence was enough to provoke an evening full of expectant silences while I tried to respond to questions about a country I had once decided to renounce.

I think now with pain and disbelief of the McCarthy era that combined with my service in Army Counter-Intelligence to put me close to abandonment of my American citizenship. My pain is all the greater because my son at twelve was as alienated from his America of the seventies as I was at twenty-four from my America of the fifties. What a terrible irony it is that I, the man who left America for three years in the mid-fifties because of its public fears and private hates, must convince the child who holds my hopes for immortality that this nation is worth his patience and his commitment.

We had come to Hardwick barely reconciled to returning to America when spring was done. Martha and I had been married in Cambridge two years before, near the end of my European tour of duty with the Counter-Intelligence Corps and just before taking up residence in Cambridge as students. Because of my mobility as a low-level agent for the CIC, I had been able to search in nine countries for the man who would allow me to write my own marriage service. After a hundred conversations that began promisingly and ended badly, no matter what the religion or the language, I found the man I was looking for in Cambridge and we had been married in his church.

He had no questions about my desire to write our marriage ceremony. Yes, he said, he had once wanted to do that himself and could understand another man's desire to do the same. But why did we want to be married abroad, thousands of miles from our families and our friends? Were we not aware that finding someone like himself was far easier in America than in Britain or on the Continent? He didn't mean to pry, he said, and he was committed to performing the ceremony in his church, if that's what I truly wanted, but he would like to know why I had chosen to be married in a country not my own.

I should have answered that I had been accepted to Christ's College, that Cambridge would be our home for the next two years, that Martha's one-way journey to England before marriage would be far less expensive than the same journey after marriage if coupled with my round trip to the States. And I could have added that the GI Bill plus army savings didn't provide for travel between England and America. I could have said all of that, but I didn't. Instead, caught in the grip of private truth, I told him of a country that could spawn and nourish a McCarthy, that could call slavery segregation, and tell the impoverished that they were merely underprivileged. That's not my country, I said.

5

I don't want to be married there. But it is your country, he said, as this one will never be.

He married us as he had promised, but twenty years have not erased from my memory the baffled, offended expression on his face as he listened to my passionate disclaimer of America. Was it the same expression I would have on my face when my son brought a small American flag to my study (a flag once sewn to a slender stick and given to children to wave at an Independence Day parade) and told me that he was going to sew it on the seat of his plants and wear it to school?

Crossing an ocean, then crossing a continent, we told ourselves that returning to America was the right choice, the only choice. For thousands of miles by ship and car we rehearsed the old arguments. After living in English poverty, could we survive American plenty? For two years we had lived on ten shillings a day, the same sum we would have in America, one dollar and forty cents between sunrise and sunrise for all that went into our mouths. Seventy cents each day for each of us bought very little, even in postwar England, and we had learned to deceive our appetites with great quantities of tea. Drunk without milk, sugar, or lemon, tea is wonderfully cheap and will often ease hunger pains that otherwise interfere with work and sleep. As we came down out of the mountains into California, wondering whether tea could be found on the frontier, our journey from one world to another nearly completed, we stopped at a roadside stand shaped and colored like a gigantic orange for two gigantic glasses of fresh orange juice. At seventy-five cents apiece, we had already overspent our entire day's food budget by a dime.

Perry Lane was a happy accident. We had rented our two-room redwood cottage by corresponding with its owners who would be absent for a year. Situated just off the northwest corner of Stanford's campus, the lane was a magnet for people like enough to form an easy community with differences great enough to preserve individual privacy. Two engineers from MIT, man and wife, living a block farther into the oak and eucalyptus, attracted to the lane by its evening action, became our friends. Not only was he the first person in our area, perhaps the first anywhere, to wire a frisbee for light, he was also well known among us for his persuasive belief in the probability of atomic war. It was he who specified the greater part of the survival kit that cost us three hundred dollars to obtain. Our contribution was to discover the mountain retreat that might make survival possible.

Does it seem mildly insane now to speak of survival kits and mountain retreats? Or to remember, in that same perfect spring, the deranged man who fired three shots from his rifle at Martha and me as we walked along Sandhill Road? After a week's hard work we had taken a long Saturday morning's walk into the brown hills behind the Stanford campus. Returning along Sandhill Road, pleasantly tired, talking quietly, I heard three times, in rapid succession, one of the few sounds that cannot be described to anyone who has not

7

heard it before. A bullet passing close to your head has
no equivalent; it is not like anything else, and cannot be
evoked by analogy. Other sounds may be more frightening: a runaway forest fire, the scream of a terrified
child—but none I know seems so indescribable as the
near passage of a bullet.

I had heard the sound once before, in a forest outside Munich when I had been following a routine
Czech border-crosser. Someone had not understood
that we were participating in a ritual that allowed the
Czech monthly access to his organization's mail-drop
and allowed me an afternoon's stroll once a month
through the German forest. He and I each recognized, tolerated, and expected the other. To this day
I want to believe that he did not know about the agent
who was following me, who shot at me and missed with
a gun that must have been the Eastern equivalent of
the .38 police special that I carried under my coat
on my hip.

That same sound had not died in my ears before I
had pushed Martha down into a roadside drainage
ditch, sometimes full in the rainy season but dust-dry
in September, told her what the sound was, and asked
her to crawl behind me. For several hundred yards we
crawled in weeds, dirt, and fear. At a culvert we huddled together for a moment, then ran for it. Only the
three shots were fired. The man, who was finally ap-
prehended after sporadic bouts of firing at hikers and
drivers, was convinced that he was shooting at Russian
communists who were infiltrating our country along
Sandhill Road. He never fired more than three times,

he explained, because he did not want to reveal his position to the enemy.

During that winter we had found employment for the next summer in two related camps in the Santa Cruz Mountains, where Martha would teach fencing and cooking to adolescents while I was teaching swimming and diving to children from six to sixteen. The two camps were built on several hundred forested acres at the top of a mountain overlooking the north end of Monterey Bay. Access to the property was fairly difficult by way of a winding road, fresh water was abundant, the forest was thick with underbrush for firewood, various buildings—some isolated—offered prospect of shelter, several orchards gave fruit, and most important, the entire property was located on the seaward and windward side of the mountain range separating the narrow coast from the inland valley that broadened into the airbases and electronic flatlands of northern California. After our summer in the Santa Cruz Mountains, we had both a survival kit and a place to survive.

Now it is easy to write that of course we never used either. To fit this new age I can recall, if I like, that we kept our kit intact for only another year even though we lived in California for three more years. I can also say that I sold the pistol at the end of the second year, having never fired it for any reason, because I could no longer believe in the reality of atomic attack and I could not tolerate the idea of defending our retreat or our small hoard of goods by shooting desperate people who lacked the foresight or good luck to be so well

9

prepared. I can and do say all of those things, but I say them largely for the benefit of my children—especially my adolescent son—so that I may rewrite personal and national history to suit both his present needs and mine. The truth, however, is more nearly this: I could have shot anyone who threatened our survival in the Santa Cruz Mountains, just as I could have shot the demented man who fired at us on Sandhill Road or the person who shot at me in the Munich woods. I sold the gun at the end of our second year in California because we had moved from Menlo Park to San Jose and saw very little of our friends who talked about war, because a gun seemed somehow ludicrous in an apartment on Tenth Street though it had seemed appropriate enough in a cottage on Perry Lane, and because we needed the money. Which is also why we removed the forty one-dollar bills and ten dollars in nickels from our hoard.

If our .38 caliber Smith and Wesson was a relatively unusual possession for domesticated Americans in the late fifties, our .22 caliber Colt Woodsman is nearly as common to American families of the early seventies as Social Security. According to Nathan Cobb, writing in the *Boston Globe* for Monday, 11 June 1973, two out of three families in the United States possess handguns. If our family is typical, then the man—himself instructed by American military marksmen in the use and care of various weapons—has instructed a reluctant woman and children in the barest essentials of killing or maiming another human being who threatens their safety. Rules like "Center the front sight in the vee of the rear sight" are combined with "Never point a gun at anyone unless you mean to use it" in a usage so dehumanized that it brings to mind Billy Graham's remarkably equal emphasis upon words like baseball and God.

A decade after selling our first pistol, we bought our second. This time the threat was far more personal than atomic war, and far easier to believe. We had bought a house in Truro, on Cape Cod, at the end of the summer of 1969. The academic year beginning in September was my first sabbatical year at Michigan. We spent that Christmas on the Cape, where I remained after the first of the year to write for several weeks while Martha returned herself and our children to their various schools. The Cape was unusually cold, snow fell frequently, and I neither saw nor heard people or automobiles unless I traveled six miles to Wellfleet to buy food or newspapers. My isolation was so complete that a walk on roads and through fields which I had walked several days earlier would reveal only the remnants of my previous footprints. Neither people nor creatures shared the Truro winter highlands with me.

No people, that is, but one. Living so entirely by myself, I kept to no normal schedule of work and sleep. Thinking in retrospect about what happened, I realized that our house must have looked to a thief or intruder no different from the many empty houses that were scattered along the highlands and through the Pamet valley. So many summer householders leave timed lights in their homes to give them some appear-

ance of occupancy during dark winter evenings that
off-season lighting-up time is a local phenomenon.
One can stand on the road near Ballston Beach at dusk
and watch the unpeopled dunes and valley come alive
with lights.

The time was exactly four A.M. by our kitchen clock.
Because our house is divided into three levels built into
the side of a hill, with the kitchen at the back on the
highest level, anyone coming upon it through the pine
forest at the rear—the most likely approach, since the
hill at the front is very steep—cannot see lights or
movement in the front room which I was using as
study and bedroom. I had just come up the stairs to the
kitchen, to set my watch which had stopped, and was
standing in front of the clock on the electric range, the
small light in the hood over the range being the only
light visible from the rear of the house, when I heard a
human cough so close that I spun toward the sound
and crouched to defend myself. Only when the cough
came again, when I had placed its source outside and
beneath the kitchen window, did I realize that the pain
in my left hand came from finger muscles constricted
around my old-fashioned pocket watch.

The training in controlled, reflexive aggression of
most American males, especially those who become
low-level intelligence agents, carried me through the
next few minutes without any conscious decisions that
I could later remember. First, my wife's favorite
kitchen utensil, a French boning knife with a strong,
narrow, very sharp six-inch blade. Then the large
flashlight aimed out the kitchen window, eight feet

12

above grade level, to illuminate the snow-covered patch of flat ground between pine forest and house. To that point it was a game of self-protection played in the isolation of winter darkness on a narrow strip of sand between Cape Cod Bay and the Atlantic Ocean. When the light found and traced in the snow one set of footprints leading from the edge of the pines to the place where they disappeared from view beneath the kitchen window, when I could no longer hope that the cough came from the throat of a deer rather than a human being, then the game never existed and self-protection became everything. As I cranked open the window, I remembered the words of the savage man who had been my CIC instructor in murder: "Any scared little kid with a gun can cancel the ticket of the toughest hand-and-knife fighter who ever lived." I had never wanted a gun as I did at that moment.

The thermometer said the outside temperature was three degrees above zero. Even with the window wide open I could feel nothing of the outside chill through the flush of fear and excitement that heated my face.

"What are you doing down there?" I spoke at nothing, my flashlight fixed on the last of the footprints I could see before they were cut off by my line of sight. Knife in right hand, flash held as far to the left of me as possible in case he tried to shoot out the light. Pure melodrama. No response came from underneath the window.

"Listen," I said, "I see your footprints and I heard your cough. If you need help, or you're just hiking through the woods, come out into the light where I can see you." Snow fell from the lower branches of a jack-pine. An owl hooted down in the valley. Suddenly I was so angry that I could barely keep my voice from shaking.

"All right, you son of a bitch, you're trespassing on my property and you can have it any way you want it. You stay right there and we'll see how bad you are." Like a man making love to his fate, I raced down two short flights of stairs, switched on the outside lights, ran across the front deck and up the hill at the side of the house. I was furious, but not furious enough to burst around the corner into the brightly lit area beneath the floodlight that shone from the top of the house. I turned the corner as widely as I could, using the nearest tree for whatever protection it could give me. I needed none. No one stood at the back of the house.

Someone had been standing under the kitchen window as I spoke through it. And whoever it was, his nerves were good, for the footprints which returned to the pines were separated from each other by the same distances separating those that led to the back of the house. He hadn't bothered to run. And the footprints were large enough to accommodate my size thirteen shoes. I didn't pursue the tracks very far into the pines. My quota of anger and bravery had been entirely used up.

Back inside the house, doors and windows locked, all outside and many inside lights giving as much illumination as I could get (this house is *occupied*), I realized how foolish I had been. Professional housebreakers do not rob houses by walking up to them at four A.M. through pine woods on mornings when the temperature is three degrees above zero. They do not even consider robbing houses that do not contain televisions, stereo hi-fi, radios, and other equipment easily fenced for relatively high prices. And, most important, professional housebreakers do not carry guns because they know they cannot shoot anybody if they do not carry a gun.

If that was no professional thief, and if he had neither identified himself nor run from the possibility of further discovery, then I shouldn't have been out there with him—flashlight, boning knife, and hand-to-hand combat training be damned. I neither slept nor wrote any more that night. When the sun had fully risen, I walked across snow-covered hills to Town Hall to speak to the Truro police.

"Crazy thing to do," the young policeman muttered as I told him the story. He wasn't talking about the trespasser. He was talking about me and I didn't like it.

"What's so crazy about it?" I asked. "What would you do if it was your property, four o'clock in the morning and you alone?"

"Get my gun," he said. "The guy has a gun, what do you do with that knife? Shit, big as you are he'd make you eat it."

"I don't own a gun," I said angrily. I'd come looking for sympathy and police protection, not for instructions from a boy.

"Well, mister, maybe you should. You gonna be up here by yourself off-season, maybe you should."

It wasn't much of an interview. I didn't like what he'd said because I knew he was right—I'd been a fool to go out there with only a knife and a flashlight. Even a big man with a knife, no matter how angry or how well trained, can be reduced to a very small size by a very small gun. I felt shrunken all during the following months whenever I recalled that cold winter's night and morning.

When we returned for the summer I was still no closer to resolving the problem. The choices seemed impossible: did I want to have a house in an area of the country where I couldn't safely live in isolation without a gun? Was there any area in any country where I could obtain such isolation as I had found on the winter Cape and still be entirely safe? Did I want to give up a house and property because I could not bear the thought of owning another gun? If violence is as American as apple pie, and handguns are as much a part of our heritage as free elections, what was I balking at? I took my story and my problem to a friend whose family has owned property on the Outer Cape for almost as many generations as the number of my summers in Wellfleet and Truro.

"Of course I have a gun," he said. "If I had known you were living up here last winter by yourself, I'd have told you to buy one. Everybody I know who spends any part of the winter up here has a pistol or a rifle. Who knows what'll come out from Boston or down from Provincetown in the middle of winter? Why take a chance?"

16

On the morning of 10 July 1970 I stopped taking chances and bought our second gun, this time a .22 caliber Colt Woodsman to shoot mid-winter intruders instead of a .38 caliber Smith and Wesson to shoot desperate victims of atomic attack. The difference in caliber came from Martha's insistence that she probably couldn't fire any gun in anger but she was sure, from what the man at the sporting goods store had said about the .38 police special, that she couldn't handle that much noise and recoil. And, besides, if our ten-year-old son Paul was to learn to shoot, it had to be with a gun that wouldn't frighten him with its sound.

Because of the nature of my Massachusetts gun permit, which allowed me to possess a gun only on my own property, I could not carry the .38 I had purchased in another town to our house in Truro. Instead, it was delivered to us late that afternoon by a young man who was kind enough to explain its operation to my wife and to give her her first shooting lesson. What provoked his kindness, I think, was my diffident answer of "a little" to his question of what I knew about guns. Though he was a very bad shot, he was reasonably knowledgeable and his intentions were so good that I saw no reason to tell him about the dozens of hours I had once spent firing various pistols at still and moving targets shaped like men. As he talked about the qualities of our Colt compared to cheap guns that were then flooding the market, I sat against a pine tree and thought about the Saturday Night Special that I had bought and sold in poolrooms

17

in two different states almost a quarter of a century before.

Very few boys I knew had guns of any description, but a lot of us carried switchblades in high school. In the late forties Baltimore had an enlightened policy of open enrollment in its high schools. Which meant that you could attend any high school in the city, no matter where you lived, simply by declaring your intention and producing your body for the formal procedures of enrollment. Distance counted for nothing to those of us determined to attend a particular school. Though a good high school was no more than a fifteen-minute walk from my home, I never considered attending it. In relation to where I lived, the school I wanted lay at the opposite end of the city's northern perimeter, half an hour of lucky hitchhiking or as much as an hour by trolley and bus. To me the inconvenience mattered not at all, for it was the high school where the heaviest gambling could be found. Following the best tradition of my neighborhood and my poolroom, I put my knife in my pocket and went where the action was.

For three years my switchblade spent most of its time in my pocket while I spent most of my time pursuing the money that comes to successful high school hustlers. At the end of three years I had almost eleven hundred dollars in winnings from campus card and crap games, pool games and bowling matches all over the city, and selected races at Pimlico racetrack. I also had a gun, part of the winnings, offered and accepted in cancellation of a fifteen-dollar debt. When the man who paid his debt with the gun took it from his pocket and placed it on top of the ten-dollar bill that was all he had to pay his twenty-five-dollar loss, I was in no position to dispute his claim that it was worth at least fifteen dollars because that's what he'd paid for it at a hock shop. It was his poolroom. The onlookers were his friends; he could have said it was worth his fifty dollars that my banker, standing next to me, was already holding, and neither one of us would have said a word. We left with sixty dollars and a loaded gun that scared us both silent.

Unloaded, together with half my winnings, the gun accompanied me to Miami Beach when I hitchhiked there with two friends after our February high school graduation. They stayed for two weeks, ran out of money, and returned home without ever knowing that I had the gun or the money. On the day they left, I spent my first of sixty-six consecutive afternoons and evenings playing cards and shooting pool. I had waited three years to find out if I could play with the best —who could always be found during the winter in Miami Beach. I carried the gun, still unloaded, in my pocket. In spite of Paul Newman's experiences in *The Hustler,* every eighteen-year-old pool player knows that broken thumbs are not the worst thing that can ever happen to you when you hustle in someone else's poolroom.

The target remained untouched as my wife fired at

19

it again and again. The children watched from the porch as their mother reluctantly prepared herself for the intruder we all hoped she'd never see. It mattered very little that she couldn't hit the target. The young man was unhappy with the results of his instruction, but I cared only that she know the feeling of a loaded gun in her hand, the powder from a cartridge exploding in its chamber. She wanted only to get done with the lesson, to get the gun out of her hand. As the bullets popped into the sand that spurted slightly with each impact, I remembered the sand that had spurted from beneath my feet as I walked mile after mile on the Florida beach—trying to understand how I had lost, attempting to decide what I should do next. I couldn't forget that half of my eleven-hundred-dollar bankroll awaited me in Baltimore.

I walked the beach for three days, sleeping for three nights on a pile of chair pads that a beachboy who was a friend of mine left on the apron of the pool at the National Hotel. I had checked out of my inexpensive hotel on the bay side of the island on the morning after the night I had come up empty, intending to keep my promise to myself to return to Baltimore if I discovered I couldn't play with the best. Then, suffering second thoughts about my ability and the money I had left with my cousin, who would send it to me if I asked for it, I checked my suitcase at the Greyhound station while I walked the beach with an unloaded gun and three one-dollar bills in my pocket. It was the gun bumping against my leg that finally convinced me I was in the wrong game. I don't think the man who bought it from me, the same man who now owned an important piece of my bankroll, had any more use for it than I did. The ten dollars he gave me, which I needed to get out of town, was simply the last gesture of the victor to the departing vanquished. For several days I missed the solid heavy presence of the gun in my pocket as I hitchhiked north to Baltimore.

Saturday Night Special, snub-nose .38, Smith and Wesson .38, Colt Woodsman .22—Miami Beach, Munich, Menlo Park, Cape Cod: handguns for poolrooms, military intelligence, atomic attack, and family safety. A gentle woman approaching middle age, having grown up in a deteriorating section of Chicago carrying a long hatpin for self-protection, returning now, twenty years later, to the same latent violence in a different form. I watched her concentrate on squeezing from the tip of her finger, locking her elbow, firing as the gun moved through the middle of the target, missing again and again before her determination overcame her dislike and the bullets first found the white background and then the black rings of the target. Her hair had fallen on her neck, her face was damp and strained, the target reasonably well perforated, our instructor ready to go home, and the worst moment could be put off no longer: now it was my turn to pass on to my son one more savage piece of his inheritance.

A year earlier, after a particularly violent episode of "Star Trek," which we often watched together with ferocious concentration no matter how unbelievable the adventure, Paul had asked me if I had really liked being a boxer. The question had been prompted by a particularly brutal and prolonged fight aboard the television spaceship that had left us both exhausted at the end of the program.

"Boxing's not like that," I said defensively, knowing what must have prompted his question.

"It hurts people. I've seen it on television and in the newspapers."

"It's true, but you don't think about it much when you do it. At least I didn't."

"Did you like it?"

"Yes, I guess I did."

"I wouldn't."

"So you won't be a boxer."

"If you liked it, how come you don't do it no more?"

"Any more. Because I'm too old and I was never very good at it. How would you like your father to have a scrambled brain as well as a scrambled nose?" I wasn't answering his real question and I knew it. How could I explain to him, nine years old, about having to fight inside because I had such a strong blink reflex that I couldn't work outside where I could see the punches coming, about having to fight inside and liking it, about covering up and moving forward until the other man ran out of ring, then working on his body until his hands started to come down and you could go for his head. About not being a headhunter like the other street kids who learned to fight in the neighborhood but then unlearned what they knew about fighting and learned to box at the Monument Street "Y" and got fancy because they thought a square with ropes was different from an alley or a schoolyard. You didn't go for the head in a street fight, so why waste your time hitting gloves and forearms and shoulders in the ring? It was a survival lesson that many of the best street fighters I knew had never learned. "Take him out with one punch" was all they could think about. They were too dumb to survive, and they didn't.

"How many of those other kind of fights did you have before you got paid?"

"You mean amateur fights?"

"Yes. How many?"

"I don't remember. Not so many."

"Did you lose all of them, too?"

A nasty question. When he'd been younger, he had insisted that losses were recorded first and victories second in reporting the results of athletic contests—so that, for example, a two and four record would mean two losses and four victories instead of its customary and invariable opposite meaning. After overhearing an impassioned, one-sided argument in which he had insisted on his odd version of the facts to a friend who knew better but who obviously did not care as much, I had waited for a private moment and told him that his friend was right.

"No," he said, "Thomas is wrong. He doesn't know."

"But he's right. Everybody puts wins first and losses second when they're talking about a sports record."

"You don't," he said, unmoved by what I had told him.

"Sure I do. Everybody does."

"You said you had a nothing-and-six record when

23

you were a fighter." Standing next to my chair, seven-year-old chin thrust forward, determination in the stance but a hint of something else in the eyes. As slow understanding of his protective, loving mistake came to me, I knew what the something else was: the fear of discovering a truth he didn't want to know. I could do nothing else but tell him.

My mother, southern born and bred, comes from a family that uses the instinctive hands-on method for communicating both affection and comfort. To touch someone lightly on the hand, forearm, or shoulder, a touch with or without words, is to speak of affection in a way that words can never do. It is also a gesture of comfort when words are inadequate or cannot be used. Paul's tightly clenched hand was inside mine as I told him that his father's record as a professional fighter had been no wins and six losses. That he had misunderstood my statement of nothing and six, that I had never won a professional fight, that someday I would explain why, but now I understood why he had made his mistake and I was glad he felt that way. We remained as we were for a long time, standing and sitting side by side, without words, his fist in mine, while he dealt for the first time with the fact that his father had been a loser. When his fist unclenched and his hand relaxed in mine, I knew and regretted the change that had taken place in our relationship. A nothing-and-six father, for whatever reason, is a hard fact for a seven-year-old to manage.

The seven-year-old was two years older, less open

but no less upset at my losses. When he struck out at me with the question about my amateur fights—Did you lose all of them too?—I was hurt and angry, but I made a mild reply and turned the conversation elsewhere. I didn't think he was old enough to handle the truth about my brief professional boxing career, and I saw no other place for the conversation to lead. Another year passed before I could bring myself to satisfy both his need and mine for talk about the difficult subjects of fighting, dishonesty, and losing.

Again we were watching television, this time a movie in which a young fighter was building a record against opposition that was barely warm. In several of his fights his manager hired opponents who would lose to apparent knock-outs in the early rounds. The action was kaleidoscopic in order to compress several years and many fights into a brief time on the screen. Paul was bored, and so was I until I realized that the action we were watching gave me the opportunity to tell him something he would have to know.

"He'll never be nothing and six," I said, referring to the all-conquering hero in the movie. Paul's eyes gleamed in the darkened room with light reflected from the television screen as he looked at me in surprise and then quickly looked away. The reference was as significant to him as it was to me. I waited, but he said nothing. Neither of us paid any attention to the fighter on the screen as we both remembered that other television show and a less happy time. Because I wanted him to ease my way with a response, and he gave me none, I put it as baldly as possible:

"Those fighters who were paid to lose. So was I. Fifty dollars a fight for six fights."

"You didn't really lose?"

"No."

"Could you have beaten them up if you'd wanted to?"

"No. Not in the ring." I had only meant to say no, and then found I couldn't. I tried to leave myself something, but he was relentless.

"You could have beaten them up if it wasn't with gloves in a ring?"

"Maybe. A couple of them. But fighting was their business and they were pretty good at it."

"Why did they pay you fifty dollars if they could beat you up? Why didn't they just beat you up and not pay you anything?"

"Because they didn't want to take any chances. Why should they take a chance with me or anybody, when fifty dollars would solve all their problems? They knew I could be bought, so they bought me." I couldn't say it any more directly than that. This time his hand was too big to be covered with mine. We sat on the sofa, separated by three feet and thirty years as he struggled to understand. While he thought about a father who had been paid to lose, I thought about how much easier it had been to throw six fights to strangers in the early fifties than to explain those six fights to my son in the late sixties.

"We don't need a gun," he had said when Martha

and I were discussing the problem of gun purchase in his presence. "You could punch 'em or use my Swiss army knife or something. We don't need a gun."

"Even your Swiss army knife wouldn't be much protection against a gun."

"But you were a fighter. Even if you did lose all your fights for money, I bet you could win if you tried." A child's faith. How much had I damaged it with the truth behind my record as a professional fighter? How much more harm would I do with this gun, these bullets, that target? I felt physically ill in the hot sun as I talked to him about weapons safety and killing for survival's sake. No one had prepared me for this dimension of being a father in mid-twentieth-century America.

My own father never fired a gun in his life or struck a blow with his fist. Too young for the first war, too old for the second, he taught nothing of violence to his sons because he had nothing to teach. A gentle man, bewildered by a world in which change was more rapid than he could follow or join, he delegated the preparation of his sons to various relatives and friends. A neighbor was the first to put boxing gloves on my fists; an over-age uncle in a civil defense group was the first to teach me to shoot. The neighbor talked about protecting myself, the uncle about protecting my country. I found myself adapting the protection formula as I spoke to my son:

"The people who make it may call it a target pistol, but that's because they want to sell guns. What it's

really meant for is protection, and I want you to learn
to use it to protect yourself and your mother and your
sister." All I left out was his country. That was another
problem.

"Will it protect us if it's only a target pistol?"

"When you point it at people, the only target they'll
be able to think about is themselves."

He liked that, repeating it to himself as he handled
the unloaded gun. His hand was already big enough
for the gun to look possible at the end of his arm.

"Can I shoot it now?"

"After you load the clip." I had intended to tell him
that I wanted him only to handle the empty gun and
clean it on the first day, which is what my uncle had
done with me. Then his question, his face, the hot
afternoon and lingering smell of powder from the
recent shooting practice—I didn't want to put him
through that, I didn't want him to become a proficient
handler of guns. Fire it. Get done with it. I gave him
the clip, watched him load it with ammunition and
place it in the gun, talked him into a comfortable firing
position, then saw him hit the target with every one of
the eight shots in the clip. He was so proud of himself;
how could I tell him that only a part of me shared his
pride, that the other part would rather he used the
pistol with the strain and distress that characterized his
mother's shooting.

"It's not so hard. That man made it seem like it was
hard. You should have taught Mom."

A pair of jays dropped out of the bright evening sky

into the darkening trees. The special light, the companionable quiet after the noise of the gun—both reminded me of Perry Lane: "I couldn't even teach her to throw a frisbee," I said irrelevantly. He let it pass as one of the aberrations of middle age.

The only extraordinary capacity I was ever able to identify in myself was the capacity for following directions. Not orders, but directions. That's not much to have to settle for when you've searched yourself with great hopes, but it's what I have and I do with it what I can. I'm not sure how it's passed from one generation to another but I have no doubt that it can be, because I've seen it in my son as well as myself. He too likes to accomplish efficient actions through the process of careful accumulation, of passing through bare, necessary means to arrive at useful and sufficient ends. He was as enthralled as I had been by the beautiful efficiency of the shooting instruction I had received in army basic training and Counter-Intelligence agents' school, and was now passing on to him. Even approximated, even carelessly followed, army small-weapons instruction can make a marksman out of the most unlikely candidate.

Paul shot well, both on that first occasion and every time thereafter that we practiced killing our enemies. Martha shot with us once more, found that she could hit the target, then found reasons for being unavailable whenever we were ready to use the gun. She and I had our first sharp disagreement about the whole mat-

29

ter of guns and protection when I bought Paul an air pistol to practice with. She wanted to know if I was preparing our son to win the same army marksmanship medals his father had won? How about planning a military career for him with a handy little gun to solve the world's problems? My response was so emphatic and inappropriate that it amazed us all:

"If we're still in Vietnam or fighting another Korea when he's drafted, I'll support him in anything he has to do to stay out."

"You've never said that before," she said. Then, thoughtfully, "I don't think you answered my questions, but it doesn't matter." She was genuinely surprised, and so was I. It wasn't the denial of her accusations that I had planned to make.

"You mean I could be a deserter and you'd help me?" We were still seated at the dinner table. Our awareness of each other was intense.

"There isn't anything you could do that would keep me from trying to help you. But it would be easier if you didn't go into the service at all because then you wouldn't have to be a deserter. I'd rather help you avoid the draft." In the Second World War we used to call them draft dodgers. No one who lived through that war could ever hear or speak that phrase again and be able to clothe it in neutral tones. Nazis, quislings, deserters, draft dodgers—a litany of despicable words for despicable human beings, among whom there were no substantial differences. Could I counsel my son to be a deserter or a draft dodger? I could do that and more.

"How could I be a draft dodger, Daddy? What would we do?" The question, the words—the conjunction of draft dodger and Daddy—so painfully innocent in a world which would give him only a little more time for such innocence. . . . I went to my study after dinner and wrote his questions together with the date at the head of a piece of paper: September 1, 1971. As I wrote it I realized that it was my brother's thirty-fifth birthday and the thirty-second anniversary of the beginning of the second war to end all wars. After which had been Korea, was Vietnam, were my eleven-year-old son's poignant questions. My answers were rooted deep in the earth that my grandparents walked upon in their journey across Europe from Kiev to Bremen and their dreadful odyssey by ship to America; in my return from England to America and to the only world that was, after all, mine; in an American university during the sixties when I sometimes advised draft-eligible students caught up in the anguish of their relationship to the war. No one had or has simple answers to those questions. I said as much to the infuriated father who came to Ann Arbor to challenge my advice to his son:

"Who are you to tell my son to be a draft dodger?" In his mid-forties perhaps, well turned-out, aggressive. His son liked him, had told me that he was a successful auto executive and a pretty good father who generally listened to his son's opinions and took them into account. Generally, but not on this issue. When he

31

had called me for an appointment, I could hear the anger in his voice; now, sitting in my office, he was still angry.

"Did you come to talk to me or to accuse me of something I didn't do?"

"Didn't do? You mean you didn't advise my son to go to Canada or some other country rather than let himself be drafted?

"I did not."

"Do you mean he's lying to me?"

"Jack's no liar. Shall I tell you what I did say to him? Then you can decide whether or not we have an argument."

I told him that I never counseled students about the draft. If what they wanted was information and advice, they could go to the draft-counseling center in Ann Arbor which would give them exhaustive, reliable information about their alternatives, and give them advice only if they asked for it. If one of my students wanted to talk about the war and his relationship to it, then I was willing and available outside of the classroom.

"All right," he said, "so it's talk you give, and not advice or counseling. Sounds to me like it comes to the same thing. When Jack *talked* to you about the war, what did you say?"

"Jack asked me what I was going to tell my son if we were still at war when he was eligible for the draft. I said I don't think it's the kind of thing you can be sure about until you have to face it, but if I felt then as I feel now I'd tell him to evade the draft and I'd help him."

"What did you say about Canada?"

"That I had met with two groups of American draft evaders during two speaking tours in Canada, and that Canada seemed to be an answer for some but not all of them."

"So you talked about draft evasion and Canada, but you didn't give Jack any advice?"

"Wrong. I talked about draft evasion and Canada and I gave Jack plenty of advice. I told him that he shouldn't make any decision without discussing it with his family, because his decision would affect everyone so deeply, and I told him not to let anyone else —including you—make the decision for him. He's the one who may have to fight and kill; he's the one who can die, not you or me or a draft counselor. He's the one who should decide."

"He's decided. At the end of next semester he gets his degree and goes to Canada. What do you think that will do to his life?" Jack's father was sitting on the edge of his chair, angry with his son and angry with me. I had neither comfort nor reassurance to give him; the young men I had met in Canada had been uniformly unhappy even if sure that their evasion and escape were justified.

"Mess it up," I said. "Anybody who says anything else is a fool or a liar. But I believe what Jack believes: that some people can mess up their lives far worse by going to Vietnam than by going to Canada."

"That's goddam treason!" He was so upset that he couldn't stay in his chair. He almost ran to the window where he stood staring at me, his hands clenched at his sides and his voice trembling with anger.

"That's goddam nonsense," I said. "A Congress that didn't declare war and keeps trying to forbid its continuance, up against a President and professional military guided by something they call our 'national honor' and not by our elected representatives. And you're so sure about what's treasonous and what isn't? You don't even recognize that a problem exists, and your son is betting his life on finding an answer."

"And when it's over? What'll happen when it's over? What'll he do, sit up there in Canada and wait for people like you to get him and his buddies an amnesty? Then he'll see what your promises are worth. Nothing! Not one goddam thing!"

"Did Jack tell you I'd promised to work for an amnesty the same way he told you I advised him to evade the draft and go to Canada?"

"It's all part of the same package, isn't it?"

"Your package, maybe. Not mine. I don't think there should be any such thing as an amnesty. Why should young men like Jack, who know what the alternatives are and can take advantage of them, be allowed to avoid what the poor and uneducated can't escape? I've told my son the same thing, and it applies to him or to Jack or to anybody else's son. Act on your conscience because you must, but don't expect the penalty to be a slap on the hand."

"You mean you'd help your son to evade the draft and then refuse to work for an amnesty? You'd stand by and watch him go to jail if he returned? I don't

34

believe it!"

"No, I wouldn't stand by and watch him go to jail. I'd do all I could to get the penalty changed to something that fits a crime of conscience better than a jail sentence."

"Like being a clerk-typist behind the lines while some poor bastard gets shot up in your place?"

"Like being legally liable for four years of service —twice the draft period—in VISTA or the Peace Corps or the Teacher Corps or any other federal agency that tries to help those who can't or don't help themselves. Four years is a long time. It's long enough to keep the cheats out and long enough to be a full repayment of service."

He stared at me for a moment, then turned abruptly and walked to the door before facing me again for his last unreconciled words: "You're both full of talk. I see where Jack gets it now. Neither one of you is willing to face the fact that anybody who isn't man enough to fight for his country doesn't have a country."

"And you're not willing to face the fact that Jack's problem has nothing to do with his manhood. You came here looking for the devil who told Jack to dodge the draft and go to Canada, and you're not willing to face the fact that there isn't any devil."

I hadn't wanted the last word, but I had it because he slammed the door as he left my office and we never saw each other again. What I had wanted was a reconciliation between Jack and his father, based upon their common recognition that the world was a different place for each of them and each had to live in his own world. What I got, instead, was a worried student coming to find out what his father had said and done.

"Did you see him after he saw me?" I asked.

"We had lunch together. He was pretty upset."

"He's got a right to be. He told me about your decision to go to Canada."

"You think I'm wrong, too?"

"What I think doesn't matter, but I don't think you're wrong. You're the one who'll have to live in Canada, not your father or me. Even so, he's got every right to be upset. He thinks that going to Canada instead of Vietnam is treason."

"So he told you that, too. When he said it to me, I told him he should join the American Legion. There he could find plenty of people who think the way he does."

The boy sitting at the other side of my desk was an intelligent, decent human being. So, I thought, was his father. Jack was no accident. If he cared enough to go to Canada, it was because his father cared enough to come to Ann Arbor to confront me. I looked away from him, through the window at the heavy flakes falling past the branches of the bare winter trees onto the ground below, snow beginning to drift against the library steps, the flagpole without its flag as barren as the ground beneath it, and realized how little I could hope to relieve their anguish. As the day diminished and lights began to outline campus walks against the snow, we talked of Canada and the boys we both knew who had chosen to leave the United States rather than submit to the draft. For the first time, as I heard the quiet sadness in Jack's voice, I thought he had begun to understand the nature of the action that he was re-solved to take.

Jack went to Canada in the late spring of 1970. A little more than a year later I found myself meeting Martha's attack on my purchase of an air pistol for Paul by claiming that I would help him to be a draft evader for wars like those in Vietnam and Korea. As we talked while sitting around the dinner table on that September evening I remembered Jack's sadness, his father's fury, my own sense of intrusion into the most private aspect of their lives, and suddenly I felt on the verge of intruding again—this time into the private life of my own son. The feeling was entirely new for me and marked a point of serious change in our relation-ship. For only the second time in our life together I consciously limited my statements of a deeply held belief so that he might have freedom to discover and shape his own views.

The first time was still painful to remember: he had come home after school, the fourth grade, so preoc-cupied with something that he had come up to join me in my study instead of greeting me and then going out to play. At first I could get nothing coherent out of him. "People say dumb things" was all he could tell me, so I agreed with him and turned back to my work.

"Daddy, do we believe in God?" The words ex-panded and reverberated in the still air of my study. My strong feelings sent a rush of words to my tongue, but I managed to keep my mouth closed after looking at my companion: nine-year-old boy built like a small fireplug, pudgy strong hands with capable fingers, scuffed worn shoes with pants patched at both knees, sweet face open and unguarded as he waited for my answer. When they came, my words were as careful and moderate as I could make them. I had never before consciously acted upon the belief that I owed him the opportunity to possess truths more valuable than inherited opinion.

"Believing in God isn't something we do together. Everybody has to decide for themselves what they believe. You may want to believe what I do now, but I want you to make up your own mind."

"Do you believe in God, Daddy?"

I had grown up in a household where our religion and our participation in it had been comfortably assumed and just as comfortably followed. My grandfather, my father's father, had been a *shamus*, a kind of lay priest or sexton in Orthodox Judaism; his wife, my grandmother, had been formidably religious in a way that he was not. My own mother, raised in a family that was committed to being Americans who worshipped as Jews rather than Jews who worshipped in America, would have little to do with the Orthodox synagogue and insisted on raising her children in the Reformed temple. As my father, with his gentle, redeeming humor, said to me when I told him that I was going to marry Martha, raised a Christian: "You're just following family tradition, son. I married further from my religion than you will from yours."

My favorite aunt had been secretary to the rabbi of

our congregation for the years of my adolescence. For most of those years I had come to meet her at the temple office late in the afternoon on Fridays from September through May, and we had gone together into the temple to attend the forty-five-minute twilight service meant primarily for, but not restricted to, mourners of the recent dead. To comfort the small number of bereaved who gathered in the temple pews, the cantor, choir, and organ sang of hope and refuge in a loving God. Though the occasion was always one of sadness, it was infused with great beauty by music and prayers. In the presence of familiar beauty I came to believe in a personal God.

Neither my aunt nor I was disturbed by the fact that I came from the poolroom to the temple. Neither of us saw any great incompatibility between the two activities, which put us directly in line with the best of my ten years of Sunday school teachers who had been able to reconcile a little ball playing in the sanctuary with a feeling of God's comfortable presence. It was she who had reminded the infuriated cantor, after he had found me in the temple having a quiet catch with a friend while we awaited our weekly Hebrew lesson with him, of the story of the juggler who had performed his best tricks before a statue of the Virgin because they were the only gifts he had to give. Though it is now thirty years ago and she is dead, I can see her face, her hand on his arm, and hear her words: "Don't be too angry with them. If only we could all be so comfortable in God's house."

My comfortable belief persisted through high

school, college, military service, marriage, teaching, and the birth of my first son. It did not endure the birth and lingering death of my second son. I asked often of that God of choirs and sanctuaries that He show Himself in the world, that He end my son's suffering by death or recovery, but He waited too long. It was then I understood that my God is busy with the Universe. I no longer look for His intervention.

How much of this could I tell Paul? I found I could not censor my feelings, could not select tender pieces of the truth in the attempt to spare his immature digestion. I told him that I do not believe in a God who knows or cares about individual people, though I do believe there may be a power that roughly shapes the universe and I am willing to call that power by the name of God. I also told him that I don't *know* anything about God and I don't think that anyone else does either, so that he or I or anyone could choose to believe whatever we wanted to believe. I said the same thing several times in several different ways because I wanted so badly for him to understand. He did, though he understood better what I felt than what I said, for when I had finished he nodded his head in agreement and said, "It's like I told them. We don't believe in God in my family."

I had spent intense, repeated moments in the intervening two years trying to retrieve my errors, and I had succeeded very little. Paul was as sure at eleven as he had been at nine that we didn't believe in God, and his "we" encompassed us all. His belief seemed to me then, as it does now, an intrusion on my part into his life. I know that the remedy for that intrusion, the eventual decision about what he will or will not believe, lies ultimately within himself. The knowledge does not make me happier with the uncareful influence I have had.

Knowing that, remembering my initial intrusion with regret, I tried to back away from Paul's response to the strong statement that Martha had provoked from me: "How could I be a draft dodger, Daddy? What could we do?" If there are no good wars, at least some are better than others. I had never wanted anything so much as I had wanted to fight in the Second World War. Fourteen years old and six feet tall, the war at full rage, my uncle in a Stateside hospital with malaria after thirty months in the jungles of New Guinea, I could not understand why I should not be allowed to be his replacement. Unknown to my parents I tried every recruiting office in the city of Baltimore. Paul might someday feel that way about another war that America would fight. Could I prepare him to evade the draft for Vietnam without permanently bending him out of the shape called American? The questions became principles that cast no shadows; my son is flesh and bone. Once more I discovered that principles, like divinities, are sometimes universal and impersonal. In their grand scale they may have little influence on the relationship between father and son.

"Evading the draft is easy if you think it's right and you're determined to do it. We could all go to live in England, for instance. We could give up our American citizenship and apply for a British passport. Since

41

Mother and I were married there and lived there, it would be easier for us than some other places."

"But why would you have to go to England? You wouldn't be a draft dodger. You were in the army."

No other conversations have ever helped me so much to know what I think as my conversations with children. Unlike adults, who are adept at hearing what you want them to hear (often in spite of what you say), children usually hear what you mean rather than what you say you mean. Until I spoke of all of us going to live in another country, I had not understood that I could not help my son to evade military service and still consider myself a citizen of the nation which, by our conspiracy, we had deprived of his service. Not until that conversation did I begin to understand the terrible strain of conflicting forces like gratitude to the country that harbors you and responsibility to the child who depends upon you. At that point, neither patriotism nor fatherhood provides a sufficient answer. For a moment I envied the easy answer that Jack's father seemed to have found.

I have read that Canada has perhaps forty thousand of our draft evaders, and that the full number in all countries, including the United States, of American men who have fled from service in Vietnam may be twice that or more. My two meetings with small groups of those men, one in western Canada and the other near Toronto, left me depressed and sick at heart. I use that phrase because the young man who arranged for me to meet with his friends near Toronto had been my Shakespeare student at the University of Michigan

and had answered my question of "How is it with you?"
with a small smile and a line from the opening scene of
Hamlet: "Tis bitter cold and I am sick at heart." Said in
the depths of a Canadian winter, even said with a small
smile and a warm handshake for greeting, the words
take on a force that leaves me with a permanent scar of
memory.

We met in a coffeehouse near the campus of the
university where I was lecturing. My former student
had written to me after he had read of my Canadian
visit in a local newspaper, had attended one of my
lectures and then taken me to the apartment of
another American draft dodger from Michigan who
was married to a local girl. There we had dinner before
the four of us drove to the coffeehouse to meet the
larger group.

Dinner was not all we had in that home on that
evening. The couple who welcomed us had been married for only six months; the refusal by his parents to
attend their wedding was still a raw sore just beneath
the married flesh of the American man and his Canadian wife. Both did their best to serve a dinner accompanied by pleasant impersonal talk, but they were too
little practiced in hiding their hurt and I was the first
American not of their generation or not fleeing from
the draft whom they had met since their marriage.
Manly, intelligent, in his middle twenties, the young
man cried openly as he spoke of rejection he could not
comprehend. To him it seemed that the same parents
who had raised him to respond first to his conscience
had refused to accept his most important application

of their training.

His tears were brief, unexpected to all of us —perhaps even to himself—and strangely unembarrassing. Because his deep emotion freed us from some of the restraints of appearance, we were able to waste less time circling the subject of amnesty. I cannot remember who mentioned it first, for all of us were thinking about it, but I cannot forget the innocent, righteous, mistaken assumption behind their initial questions. Who were the individuals doing the best work in behalf of a general amnesty, and what groups were most effective? What were student and faculty activists at the university doing to bring pressure to bear on Nixon's hard-line position? Did I have any ideas about what they might do from a distance to help themselves?

Having eaten their food, sitting at their table, I told them I felt like Judas should have felt at the Last Supper. Then I explained that I couldn't answer their questions very well because I hadn't paid much attention to the amnesty movement. I had paid so little attention to people and organizations in the movement because I thought they were wrong. Utterly wrong. As I added the last two words of emphasis, I realized how unnecessary they had been. My three companions had become so still that I could not see or hear them breathe.

"You don't believe in amnesty?" The Canadian woman spoke, shock in her eyes, in the shape of her mouth, in her words. She leaned toward me across the small table, as though to be sure of my presence as well as my reply.

"If you mean total amnesty, no, I don't. I think that amnesty should be limited to guaranteeing freedom from criminal prosecution and I think it should require every draft evader to give four years of national service in some peaceful, productive, demanding way."

"But if the war is wrong, and almost everybody in America seems to think it is, then we're right. Why should we have to pay any penalty if we're right?"

We carried the argument with us to the coffeehouse where we met five more refugee Americans, one of whom had brought a wife across the border with him. It was he who astounded his companions by taking my side of the dispute.

"If you're ready to stay here for the rest of your life, then it doesn't matter," he told them. "You could afford to hold out for a general amnesty because you'd be all right if you never saw America again. But I wouldn't be. Someday I've got to go back. It's where I live."

It's where I live. The words lay with such size and weight among half-eaten doughnuts and cold cups of coffee that they seemed to leave no room for anything else. Beneath their weight the group's conversation hesitated, staggered a brief way, then collapsed through shrinking phrases into silence. It's where I live. None of us had more, or less, to say.

Their faces were as clear and present to me when I spoke with my son on a September evening in Ann Arbor as they had been in that winter coffeehouse in

Toronto. Only a generation of violent fathers could have so utterly displaced those sons, could have reduced them to unfounded hopes for amnesty, understanding, welcome, forgiveness. We had filed slowly out of the coffeehouse into the parking lot where we had dispersed to our cars, handshakes all around but eyes shielded and inward-looking, each seeing only himself. I can set no limit on the price I am willing to pay that my son may never find himself in their circumstances.

Peace
and the
Flag of
War...

Peace and poverty had been America's portion in the thirties, and my family had lived with a fair measure of each. Our relative poverty would be more important to me during my adolescence, when I would try to remedy it by gambling on pool, cards, bowling, horses—anywhere I could find an edge and get down a bet. But during my childhood it meant very little, especially by comparison to the peace in which my family and my country allowed me to flourish.

Peaceful seems to me now to have been the dominant feeling of my early years. When the summer nights were unbearably hot, we would take blankets to a neighborhood park and sleep in the imagined coolness of imaginary breezes from a nearby reservoir. It mattered not at all that we did not recognize the family settled two yards to our right, the young couple with their heads together stretched on their stomachs at our feet, or the single man smoking with his back against a tree. Had you told us he was a convicted murderer who had served his time, we would not have worried about our safety. We had not yet developed the wary jungle habits of modern city beasts.

The basement that came with our rented first-floor apartment—we got the basement; the people on the second floor got the breeze—was home to an unbroken succession of stray dogs who adopted my father during his daily collection rounds as an insurance agent. They might stay for a few days or weeks or even for a few months, but inevitably my mother would refuse to take care of them any longer and my father would have to take them elsewhere, even if that meant the Humane Society. But dogs were only half the stray life in our household. Especially after we moved to our own two-story row home, beggars and peddlers of every tongue and dress were as frequent in our kitchen and on our back porch as dogs had been in the basement of our apartment. We were the local watering hole for every stray human who passed through our neighborhood, some of whom were rough-looking by any standards. In twenty-six years of resolute and undiscriminating charity, my fearless mother says she did not experience a single

50

unpleasant word, much less a threatening action. Today she finds those facts so commonplace that they seem to her not to be worth remarking. As she once told me, "They *knew* I expected them to be nice."

Her expectations, I came to understand, were the primary force in her relationships with Baltimore's strays. Those same expectations had enormous influence upon her children, not perhaps so much in what they did but in what they expected of others. From my eleventh year, soon after we moved from rented apartment to purchased home (fifty dollars down payment, two weeks vacation pay for my father from the insurance company), I wandered over the entire city, spending more and more of my time in that area of Baltimore which runs to the waterfront where my father and his family had landed in America some forty years before.

I returned to the Baltimore docks because I felt more comfortable there than anywhere else in the city. The dark smell of the water, rotted pilings and rusted ships, unshaven men who wore wool hats even in summer, cobbled streets with horse-drawn wagons amid the great dockside tangle of trucks, cars, people—especially the people. I felt with them the sense of repose my mother must have felt with the strays in her kitchen and on her porch. In four years on the docks and in the streets of the dockside area, I was never seriously mistreated. Like my mother, I think I carried with me a peace that was contagious.

Was that peace only an individual and familial gift, an inherited personal environment, or was it a national possession as well? In 1930 we had not been at war for a dozen years and would not be again for almost an equal period. In 1960, when my first son was born, we were within five years of having fought in Korea and having occupied West Germany. Far worse for the peace that would be no part of my son's inheritance, the year of his birth was also the first year of our "presence" in Vietnam.

No one can yet know what our decade of war in Indochina has meant to our national spirit or, closely related, to our estimate of ourselves. For the first time in this century, the quality of our humanity is on trial and we are the judges. We have lost a war, which is something; but, much worse, we have lost a part of our self-esteem, which is everything. What this will mean on a national or international level, I can only guess. But I do not have to guess at what it has meant to Paul and me as we have played our roles, thirty years apart, of inheritors. In the course of those three decades, a single generation in the life of our family, America and her symbols have come to signify values and acts that only recently were far different in meaning:

Derek was a retired merchant seaman whose daily responsibilities on the Baltimore waterfront included raising and lowering a large American flag. He was born an Englishman, having served in the British navy in the First World War when he had come on a naval mission to America and found that America fitted him. After the war he returned here as soon as he could and joined the Merchant Marine, eventually becoming a citizen of the United States, finally retiring to live with his sister in Baltimore. He was the first person I knew who drank tea and spoke English with an accent that wasn't German or Middle European. For years I thought that "British accent" described a speech like Derek's broad Cockney, and that tea had to be so dark and thick that you filled your cup half full of milk and then chewed it like molasses as it flowed slowly past your teeth.

Derek's flagpole is gone and urban renewal has so altered the dockside area that I am now unsure of its exact location. But I am certain of how much he cared about that flag, how concerned he was to teach me his knowledge and tell me his feelings. Though the waterfront was many miles through the city from my home, I managed to be there several times a week for four years to help him raise or lower his flag.

Derek knew just how to fold the flag into its proper tricorn shape, a shape which he especially valued, he said, because it reminded him of the common history shared by England and America. Today, thirty years and more after the event, I can recall how it felt to carry the tightly folded flag to the flagpole and to help it into the air while Derek hauled upon the lines. On my thirteenth birthday, for the first time, he let me handle the lines while he held the flag. I remember how I felt when he said he thought I was man enough for the job.

In a climate of opinion so profoundly changed as that in America between 1943 and 1973, it seems necessary to say that Derek was a simple, kind man, proud of his adopted country and dismayed at the ignorance of its history displayed by most of its citizens. When he would not allow me to hoist the flag until I was thirteen, he was being true to his vision of a man's work. When I explained to him that I was to undergo the Jewish initiation ceremony called "bar mitzvah" on the Saturday after my thirteenth birthday, and that thereafter I would be regarded in the Jewish tradition as a man responsible for his own acts, he responded with his own ritual recognition of manhood by allowing me to raise the flag for the first time.

For a year before that dark Saturday morning in January of 1943, almost exactly coincident with the time I had been taking weekly Hebrew lessons at the temple so that I could read from the Torah, I had been instructed by Derek in his private catechism of the flag. To this day the flag means more to me, I think, because I know so much about it.

According to Derek, anyone who lives in a country with a red, white, and blue flag is responsible for knowing why the flag is composed of those colors. How many times did I recite for him that red was for valor, white for purity, and blue for both vigilance and justice? I remember my surprise at hearing the word "valor" when he first used it. I had thought it was a word unused after King Arthur and his knights of the Round Table.

Derek was especially proud that the first flag truly representative of revolutionaries in all the colonies was the Grand Union Flag first raised by a man like him-

54

self, a seaman named John Paul Jones, in December of 1775. This was the same flag that George Washington used one month later, thirteen alternate red and white stripes (more red than white, said Derek, because valor was a little more important than purity) with the crosses of Saint Andrew and Saint George against a blue field.

When he discovered that I had never heard of either saint, he was shocked into a morning's silence. I tried to explain that Jews didn't have saints, or at least I didn't think they did, but he wasn't to be so easily appeased. For the first time he questioned me closely about what kind of people Jews were that they didn't have saints, which was a hard question to answer, and what kind of school I went to that I could spend so much time with him and others down on the docks? The first question may have been hard, but the second was dangerous. The expression on my face must have told him more than he wanted to know because he never asked me about school again. Instead, he proceeded to teach me what he knew about the flag, slipping in a little information about saints when he judged his question about school to be forgotten.

In Derek's opinion, the least understandable action his adopted country had ever taken was to substitute a constellation of stars, each representing one of the United States, for the combined crosses of George and Andrew, patron saints of England and Scotland respectively. To remove that symbol of union between two English-speaking countries from its conjunction with the thirteen stripes, symbol of the union of thirteen English-speaking colonies, was Derek's idea of a leviathan drowned before it was born. That was the image he used. Having already made the mistake of inquiring about George and Andrew, I made no such mistake about leviathan. Being more a land animal than Derek, who was irretrievably part of the sea, I had some trouble with the idea even after I had read about leviathan in an encyclopedia, but I never questioned him about it. One morning's silence as a mark of my ignorance was enough.

In addition to December 1775 and January 1776, Derek demanded that I learn three other dates and their attendant events before he would allow me to raise the flag. The first was 14 June 1777, the day on which Congress resolved that our flag should be thirteen red and white stripes with thirteen white stars on a blue background; the second was 4 April 1818, the date on which Congress declared that the way to recognize an expanding union was not to add stripes but to add stars to the flag. In between those two was the date we both cared most about, for it was as near to our hearts as the Chesapeake Bay soft-shelled crab.

Baltimore schoolchildren may now grow up without venerating local heroes, but if they do I'm sorry for them and sorry for the impoverished world they create in their image. Who, if he had the choice, would not want to know about Francis Scott Key, Edgar Allan Poe, H. L. Mencken, and George Herman Ruth? I may have been familiar with the Baltimore Babe before I was born to this life, and I learned about Poe and Mencken soon thereafter, but I owe my first acquain-

56

tance with Francis Scott Key to Derek's appetite for information about the flag and his affection for anything that had to do with the sea.

It was Derek who taught me that the history of my native country, his adopted land, does not have to be experienced solely through books, that it is a vital history which can generate high excitement for anyone with maximum curiosity and minimum funds. My first personal discovery of an America that was not limited to the short span of my lifetime was the discovery of Francis Scott Key, Fort McHenry, and the fifteen-striped, fifteen-starred flag whose gallant streaming over that Baltimore harbor fort had provoked Key to write "The Star-Spangled Banner."

Anyone trained by Derek would know for the rest of his life that the American flag with fifteen of both (recognizing the later admission to the Union of Vermont and Kentucky) flew over our country from 1795 until 1818. He would also know that Key was a Marylander born and bred who was kept overnight on a British vessel anchored in Baltimore harbor, after he had boarded it to seek the release of a friend, because the British were taking no chances on his discretion and their plans to shell the fort. When morning came and Key saw the flag still floating high above McHenry, he could do no less in his pride than compose a poem to commemorate its survival. The date was 14 September 1814.

Derek declared that living a century and a half after the shelling of the fort was a mere accident in time, and that we did not have to be governed by accidents. It was true, he said, that we were handicapped because we couldn't shell the fort overnight and expect to remain free long enough to view anything in the dawn's early light. But he did have a friend who was owner and captain of one of the working boats in the harbor, and that friend might be willing to take us around the point next Saturday morning so that we could see Fort McHenry from the same position that Key must have seen it from the deck of a British ship.

Saturday was the only morning possible for Derek. During the week he had other duties between raising and lowering the flag, and he spent Sunday morning with his sister in church. On Saturday, however, his only responsibility was to the flag; he was free between raising it at eight in the morning and lowering it at five in the evening. But if Saturday was good for him, it was bad for me. I could leave home as early as I liked on school mornings because my father was always up and out before seven, sometimes before six, and I could have my breakfast with him. Since both he and my mother were entirely innocent of what really went on in American public schools, any reasonable invention about very early school activities was enough to put me beyond suspicion for weekday departures at any hour.

Saturday was another problem. Because our home was an hour's ride by trolley through the city to the waterfront, I could leave no later than seven in order to be beside the flagpole at eight. Even lucky hitchhiking combined with running never took less than forty-five minutes. My parents didn't know much about being twelve years old in America in 1942, but they knew enough to know that nobody was out playing ball before the sun was up. Finally I had to use my uncle who lived nearby and was just a few years too old, to his lifelong regret, to go to war. In order to use him—he drove his car downtown on Saturday mornings, parking it about a mile from the docks by seven thirty—I had to tell him the truth since I couldn't think of a plausible lie that was likely to satisfy him. Though I knew him well, I was unprepared for his response.

"Why don't you want to tell your mother and father?"

"Because they wouldn't understand."

"You mean because they would understand. You don't go to school much, do you?"

"Not much."

"You spend a lot of time down on the docks?"

"Some. Not so much."

"Are you thinking about shipping out when you're old enough?"

"No. Well, maybe. I just sort of like it down there. You can learn about things."

"Like what?"

I told him what Derek had taught me about the flag. I threw in all the saints and leviathans and revolutionary heroes I could think of. I spoke about colors and constellations and stripes. I recited dates and places. Only after I wound up with Francis Scott Key at Fort McHenry, and the adventure that Derek and I could have on Saturday, did I realize that I had spilled it all

59

after a year of telling no one, not even my friends. If he wanted me, he had me. He could ruin the whole thing by telling my parents.

"Here's a dollar."

"For what?"

"For trolley fare. I don't want you hitchhiking down-town. With the war bringing new people into town, it's not safe like it used to be. When you've spent that one, tell me and I'll give you another. And I'll tell your mother I'm taking you to work with me Saturday morning because I need your help."

That was how I found myself aboard a small harbor tug at eight thirty the next Saturday morning, more excited than I had ever been in my life. We were going out to anchor where we thought the British vessel must have sat awaiting nightfall and the opportunity to blow Fort McHenry and Old Glory right off the hill. In the mist and soft autumn light, it was possible to imagine anything at all. The great ship that slid past on our starboard side might have been a British frigate; the orange mist might have been colored in part by ex-ploding powder instead of entirely by a rising sun. I fingered the eighteen nickels in my pocket—I had used two from my uncle's dollar on trolley rides during the week—and thought myself prepared for any ad-venture.

Whatever else I was prepared for, it was not the old fort with its flag still guarding Baltimore harbor. We had sailed southeast from the municipal piers at the head of the northwest branch of the Patapsco River, out into the main road of the great river itself. The sun shone over our port side until we were fairly out of the mouth of the branch and had turned our stern to the southeast so that we could see the fort just as Key must have seen it on that September morning in the early nineteenth century. As the mist lifted and the fort with its flag came into clear view, I felt like I was looking at all of America. In thirty years since that day, very few sights have so filled my eyes.

We could stay only briefly, for the captain had Saturday shipboard maintenance to do, but briefly was enough for Derek and me. The sight had left us wordless, and we returned to our pier with no more than monosyllables between us. Our talk and our reading had prepared us so well that the actual sight had been like placing the keystone in an arch, the last and necessary act before all that precedes it can bear the full weight of meaning. Prolonged gazing was no more to the purpose than extended talk.

Back at the corner of Pratt and Light streets, we found ourselves with a single thought: the day was still new, the air clear and warm, Fort McHenry seen only from its seaward side. What was to keep us from coming upon it by land? I felt the weight of nickels in my pocket and for the first time knew the mobility of wealth. I might as well have fingered dross for all the use my fortune would be to me that day.

Since his mustering out from the Merchant Marine, Derek had never used any transportation but his feet on dry land. Because we had been nowhere together but to the front of his sister's house, where I had walked with him several times after flag lowering, I did not know that Derek went only where he could walk or travel by ship. As he told me when we set out due south on Light Street, it was but a three-mile stroll to the face of the fort.

I have since measured on a map the distance south on Light and east on Fort Street, and it is three miles. I suppose he could have measured it too, just as I did so many years later, but I prefer to believe that Derek had a special sense of dead reckoning peculiar to seafarers, even as he had a special appreciation for America that sometimes comes with late and loving discovery. The three miles were nothing as he described to me what I would see.

When we arrived at the fort and looked out over its battlements, my mind was so fully furnished with the great figures and events of America's first fifty years as a nation that I was shocked at the physical reality of the ships that lay in Patapsco water. Derek's own vital sense of the Revolutionary era had supplied so much contemporary life to my imagination that some part of me expected to hear cries in the shrouds of full-rigged ships of war. I turned my face away from Derek, keeping it averted from him for shame that he would see the tears in my eyes as I mourned a time I would never know and men I would not see.

I have no memory of the early part of our walk back to the waterfront. I was dazzled by history, by the making of a nation and the part my native city had played in confirming my country's existence. For the first time I understood some of the meaning of union, and something more of the feeling of being American.

Though Derek and I were to walk the city together for two more years, searching for and finding America while war shattered the England he had left and the Russia my father's family had abandoned, I was never so moved again by discovery as I was during that fine autumn morning at Fort McHenry. Not George Washington's great statue in Mt. Vernon Place, the first monument raised to him in America; nor St. Mary's Industrial School, Babe Ruth's orphanage; nor Edgar Allan Poe's grave; nor H. L. Mencken's columns read in the depths of the Enoch Pratt Free Library —none of these nor dozens of others worked upon my imagination or my emotions as had that bare fort on a green rise with dark water at its foot and a flag at its head. Which may explain some part of the depth of my reaction, thirty years later, to my son's intention to dishonor that flag.

How could I tell Paul of Derek, his flag, an old tug in Baltimore harbor, and an autumn morning thirty years past when he came to the door of my study to show me the small American flag he intended to sew on his jeans? I could feel my face heat with anger as his fingers spread the colors across the seat of his pants.

"Look, Dad. I'm going to sew it here and wear it to school."

Had I wanted to interpret them, many signs would have led me to anticipate the moment. Had I wanted to know, I could have known that this sweet-natured, intelligent boy who had been such a continuous joy to live with, would confront my unspoken, deeply felt patriotism with his own generation's discomfort and

63

disgust. But I had chosen not to read the signs he had left for me. Now, as I watched him spread the flag across his buttocks, I felt impossibly fragmented, broken and scattered by love of child and country, terrible anger, rising despair. Would the sight have been more bearable had I not recognized the tattered rectangle as a remnant from a Fourth of July parade during his early childhood? Then he had sat upon my shoulders and waved his small flag exuberantly, perhaps even proudly, at floats and marching bands as they passed on the street.

As Paul approached his eleventh birthday we had increased the number of our season tickets to the Michigan basketball games to include a seat for him, and he had taken the opportunity to tell me something about himself that I had refused to notice for many months before. The occasion was the first Big Ten game of the year, the visiting team appearing to be almost as incompetent as ours in pre-game drills. Maybe they're bad enough for us to win, I said to him as we stood for the playing of "The Star-Spangled Banner," and the thought moved me to sing the song's lyrics with special enthusiasm while the band played and lights shone on the great flag above our heads. Sometime during the song I noticed two things simultaneously: Paul was not singing and he was staring at me with an odd frown on his face, quickly hidden when he realized that I was returning his stare. I put the information away for the duration of the game, but every instinct told me of the emotions that lay behind his troubled eyes and mouth.

Peace and the Flag of War

Having come without family or friend to occupy our third seat, only the two of us had to agree that the half-time show by the gymnastics team had been the high point of the evening's entertainment and that we should leave before we became permanently alienated from college basketball. Soon after the second half began, we left the arena to stand under cold stars on a winter's night perfect for the twenty-minute walk to our home. It was a lovely night for walking but no night at all for confronting the complex question that had come between us during the playing of the anthem. Our ritual discussion of the coach and his players lasted only a block or two. I asked the question before the exhilaration of silence and winter's chill made serious talk impossible:

"Do you know the words to 'The Star-Spangled Banner'?"

"Not all of them."

"Only Francis Scott Key knew all of them. How about the words to the first stanza, the words I was singing tonight? Do you know those?"

"Most of them."

"You weren't singing them. Don't you like the song?"

"No. It's a war song. I don't want to sing it."

The rhythmic pounding of our boots on the pavement could not have been mistaken for the sound of marching jackboots by any listener. Behind the doors of the modest homes we passed—the one we had lived in several years ago would soon be on our left—were people who hated war, who would not create or long bear the self-creation of a *Führer* to lead them into genocide at home or abroad. Of course it was a war song, celebrating a perilous fight, ramparts, rockets, bombs bursting. . . . "You're right. It is a war song. In fact it's got a couple of lines in the third stanza that make fights and rockets and bombs seem pretty tame stuff. For instance, how do you like 'their blood has washed out their foul footsteps' pollution'?"

"I hate it. It's really icky."

"So do most people, I guess. Maybe that's why nobody sings those stanzas. Most people probably feel more or less like you do."

"So why does everybody sing the first part?"

"I sing it because I like the country that the flag stands for, so I don't care a lot about the words."

"Well I do. Why couldn't we sing another song? Like 'America the Beautiful' or something?"

"I like that too. But it's not our national anthem."

"Sure. Because we like war songs better. We're always killing people somewhere, so that's why we like that song."

"That's unfair and you know it. Do you think of God every time you say 'gosh' or 'golly'?"

"What does that mean?"

"It means that words like 'gosh' and 'golly' are just forms of the word 'God'. At least that's what they were when people started saying them because they felt uncomfortable about saying 'God' all the time. Like you say 'geez' or 'gee whiz' instead of 'Jesus' or 'Jesus Christ'. Except 'gosh' and 'golly' and 'geez' are only words now, and nobody thinks of 'God' or 'Jesus' when

66

they say them. Just like I don't think of 'The Star-Spangled Banner' as a war song when I sing it. And I'll bet there aren't many people who do."

"Then why are we always fighting wars everywhere and killing people?" He paused, then had the last word: "Anyway, you don't sing the tune so good."

We both smiled. Part of his being a joy to live with has always been the redemptive timing of his humor. We were just abreast of the house in which he had celebrated his second and third birthdays. I laughed aloud as the house reminded me of the time during our residence in it that he had told me, chubby and very earnest, when I had made, up some nonsense about our food floating out the open kitchen window because it was such a light lunch we couldn't keep it on the table, that we could make jokes about everything but not about eating. Food, he said, with great seriousness, was not for being funny.

Nor was the anthem, the pompous ass in me thought but did not say, moved by memory of his early childhood to glance covertly at the profile that bobbed along at my shoulder. Whenever I noticeably slowed my normal stride, he would complain that I was treating him like a little boy or I wasn't "stretching" him, his word for the effort he had to make to keep up with me. Now I felt the obligation to stretch him in a different and more dangerous way, but the greater peril seemed to lie in letting the moment pass with a small joke and a companionable smile. I plunged in:

"Do you know the words to the pledge to the flag?"

"Sure. 'I pledge allegiance . . .'"

"I believe you. Do you say it when you get the chance in school or somewhere else?"

"In school. Sure I do." A silence, followed by a puzzled expression and a question: "What's that got to do with singing 'The Star-Spangled Banner'? The pledge doesn't say anything about war, does it?"

"No, but it does say some things that other people don't like as much as you don't like 'The Star-Spangled Banner.' " I watched his lips move as he repeated the pledge to himself, the puzzlement clear on his face.

"Like what things? I just said it all the way through and I don't see anything not to like."

"How about the last six words?" He looked so blank that I made the mistake of quoting them: "You know, 'with liberty and justice for all'." His face flushed; he knew when he'd been patronized.

"Do you think I'm dumb or something? I know the words. But I don't see what's not to like about that."

"A teacher lost her job last year in New York State because she thinks those words are so wrong she can't bring herself to say a pledge that ends with them." I told him as much as I knew then of Susan Russo who had found herself unable in good conscience to voice the pledge to the flag which was used to open each school day in Henrietta, a small town outside of Rochester, New York, where she had gotten her first job as a high school art teacher. My knowledge of her plight had come from a related case in Michigan. While visiting in Rochester I had described the Michigan incident to a friend and he had drawn parallels with the Russo case in questions of individual liber-

68

ties and community rights. Paul's initial reaction was in part like mine.

"You mean she wouldn't say the pledge because she didn't think everybody in America got liberty and justice? Well, I think that's a pretty good reason. I just never thought about it before."

"Do you think she had a right not to say it in school if she didn't want to?"

"Sure. I know kids who don't say it because it says 'under God' and they don't believe in God. Teachers shouldn't have to say it either if they don't want to."

"I say it when I get the chance, and I don't believe in God very much. Sometimes I just leave those two words out. And I know a whole lot about liberty and justice in America being only for some people, mostly white people who can afford it, but I say the pledge anyway because I want to make it come true for everybody. Do you think I should stop saying it?"

"No. You can say it if you want to."

"Are you going to say it?"

"Yes, I guess so."

"You've got a right to make up your own mind about that. And I want you to let me make up my own mind about singing 'The Star-Spangled Banner.' I'll let you do the same."

"I'm not going to sing any war song."

"So don't. But don't be angry when I do or somebody else does."

We marched on, both of us being stretched several different ways. I realized with regret that Fort McHenry could never mean to him what it had meant

69

to me. I had saved it for him, waiting for the best moment to give it, and I had waited too long. Some gifts cannot wait a generation for giving.

"There was another thing about that teacher being fired from her job." He had been concentrating on keeping up with me, on the physical pleasure of using his lengthening legs to stride like a man. He frowned as my voice penetrated the hood of his parka. Obviously he would rather walk than talk, but a child's desire not to be instructed can have little effect on a father who is also a teacher. "Sometimes I think she was fired because she should have been fired."

"Because she wouldn't say the pledge she should have been fired? I don't think that's right."

"No, neither do I. But what we think may not be as important as what the parents of the community think."

"So she should say the pledge because they want her to even if she doesn't want to?"

"I didn't say that. But maybe she shouldn't teach in a community where parents want teachers to say the pledge as an example for their children. She's got every right not to say the pledge, but maybe she doesn't have the right to take a job where she knows they will want her to say it."

"Suppose she didn't know they wanted it."

"That's a hard question. If she didn't know it when she took the job, she found out pretty soon. Should she resign then because parents have a right to say who sets what kind of example for their children? How much right do they have?" I was asking myself questions I couldn't answer, questions not intended for my eleven-year-old companion who, not knowing that, answered them anyway.

"I wish we had one like her in our school. Seeing her not say the pledge or salute the flag would really show me something." He paused and then almost to himself he said, "But I'd say it anyway." It was an answer, I thought, as we turned the corner toward home, that I needed to hear—no matter what beliefs and attitudes I professed. And if some part of my son said it because he thought his father needed to hear it, that was all right too.

This son who would not sing the anthem but who would say the pledge to the flag stood at the door to my study and held that same flag (to which he would pledge his allegiance) across the seat of his pants, in the place where he intended to sew it and sit on it, and waited for my response. In a mechanical, mindless attempt to control the sudden fury that made my hands clench and sweat—fury at his light voice, his quick fingers stretching the thin material of the flag against denim pants, his pleased smile—I found myself counting the thirteen stripes on the tattered flag, then the fifty stars still bright against their blue field. The counting was useless; my face and eyes burned as though I had a fever. For a terrible moment that will remain with me for the rest of my life, I looked upon my son as my enemy. I would have struck him with my fist had he stood within reach.

Anger took such complete possession of me that I could not speak. I was hardly aware that the telephone was ringing until Paul walked into my study and picked up the receiver, flag in his other hand, standing next to my chair where I could easily reach him. To protect us both, I swiveled my chair toward the window as he spoke to the caller, his friend. Had the call been for me, I could not have spoken. The pounding in my ears made Paul's voice sound distant and insubstantial as I stared through my window at children playing on the sidewalk below. If I could not deal with the present, I could at least submerge it in the past:

Derek was a small man of considerable strength, in age somewhere between my father and grandfather, who passionately hated all French sailors, whom he called "frogs." Since Baltimore was one of the favorite ports of leave for Allied ships sailing the Atlantic, there were plenty of French sailors to feed Derek's passion. Convinced that no Frenchman could understand English, since he was certain that no self-respecting Englishman could understand French, he never bothered to lower his voice as he slandered the parents of all Frenchmen who passed on the street. Though I had never seen it happen, the occasional condition of his face and knuckles led me to believe that at least some Frenchmen must understand at least a little English.

One fine spring morning the worst thing happened. Only a genius who was also a devil could have thought of it; as a form of revenge upon Derek, it was inspired and malevolent. During the night someone had shinnied up Derek's flagpole, attached a large French flag, then cut and removed all the hoisting lines. In itself this would have been enough to drive Derek into wild anger until he had removed the offending flag, but it was not enough for the devil who conceived it. The touch of evil genius was the heavy grease that coated the flagpole from top to base, grease so thick and slippery that nothing human could ascend the pole to remove the flag that flew from its peak.

Had the grease not been there, Derek would have shinnied up his flagpole and the French colors would have lasted no longer than the time it took him to reach the top of the pole. With the pole unclimbable, the flag blowing nicely in the harbor breeze, Derek nearly insane with rage and frustration, people gathering from all over our area of the docks, a photographer said to be on his way from the *Baltimore Sun* to make a permanent record of Derek's anguish and a Frenchman's genius, I decided there were better places to be truant than in the middle of an international incident, which is what the angry woman who owned the nearby lunchroom called it again and again. I knew if my picture appeared in the paper, I'd be a local incident of painful importance.

I didn't feel happy about leaving Derek but I didn't know what else I could do for him after I'd ruined my school clothes by repeatedly trying and failing to climb that greasy pole. After the first few minutes I don't think he knew I was there as he swore and raved at the French, their flag, and the animals who had done this to his pole. That evening, a Friday, I was at the door waiting for my father to bring home the *Evening Sun* with its pictures of the flagpole and Derek. There was nothing. I went through every item on every page of that paper, of both the morning and evening papers on Saturday, and of Sunday's huge edition. Nothing. Not a word. I couldn't believe it. An international incident involving our flag during wartime, and the newspaper didn't even mention it! I was outraged; because it was a weekend, I was also helpless. My family had plans that included me, Derek and his sister didn't have a telephone, and I was unable to get down-town to the docks to find out the truth for myself. Monday morning was desperately slow in coming.

During the long weekend I decided to take the chance, dangerous though it was, of being absent from school on consecutive mornings. Junior high school, I had discovered in my first year, was a new experience in one important respect: it had a truant officer who was almost certain to call your home if you missed school two mornings in succession. In the fifth grade I had found the weak point in the walls of the community jail known as grammar school: nobody thought that an eleven-year-old boy would go anyplace but to school on weekdays between September and June, and nobody believed that the same boy could produce notes in his mother's or father's handwriting upon demand. The discovery meant freedom for me in the second half of the fifth grade and all of the sixth, but careless rapture turned to careful planning when I discovered the suspicious nature of junior high school administrators. To keep them from snapping at my heels, I found I had to show up for morning homeroom roll call at least every other day. Then, if there were better things to do, the nurse was susceptible to open-mouthed, pop-eyed imitations of an asthma sufferer. Considerable practice brought me to the point where I could wheeze as convincingly as my brother, who really did have asthma.

But no matter how inspired my wheeze might be on Monday, it couldn't get me downtown in time to raise the flag with Derek if I went to school first. At seven forty-five by the clock in the lunchroom, in spite of whatever the truant officer and my parents might do to me, I was running around the corner toward the door that Derek would come out of with the flag. Walking toward me, carrying Derek's flag, was a very large man I had never seen before in my life. I was so astounded that I ran into him.

"Easy there, boy. Watch where you're going."

"Are you carrying the flag for Derek?" Because I had left him when he was desperate for help, he had replaced me with this man. I was ready to fight him for the flag.

"Who's Derek?"

"What do you mean, who's Derek? He's the man who raises the flag."

"Little guy who talks funny?"

I wanted to punch him in his fat mouth. He didn't look like he could run much. It hurt me to acknowledge that in anybody's eyes Derek might be a little guy who talked funny. I looked away and slightly nodded my head.

"He had some kinda accident last week. He's home

sick now, so I got to do his job and mine too. Friend of yours?" I barely caught the last question over my shoulder. I ran the whole seventeen blocks to Derek's house.

I should have known that fat mouth would have the wrong information—Derek was in the hospital, his sister told me over a cup of tea in her sitting room. She was a pleasant-spoken, gentle woman who was deeply worried about her brother. After her story, so was I. Derek had never come home from the docks after the violation of his flagpole. While watching the French colors being removed by a hook and ladder company, he had fallen heavily to the ground though no one was near who could have pushed him. He was kept from falling again by the lady from the corner lunchroom who noticed the odd working of his mouth, his wild gesticulations and rubber legs, and held him against her large body until he fainted and went limp in her arms. Closing her lunchroom, she had taken him to the hospital in a taxi, stayed with him as long as she could, then come to his home to notify his sister that Derek had suffered a stroke.

Because his sister had given me the room number, I didn't have to stop at the hospital's information desk before entering the elevator—which was just as well since several signs said clearly that children under fourteen were not allowed above the lobby floor. When I had spoken with her for the first time on Monday in her parlor, she knew only that the doctors were cautiously favoring small permanent effects when she had finally abandoned her hospital vigil of sixty hours. She had guessed that he might be able to have visitors by the end of the week. Almost to the hour a week had elapsed since our discovery of the French flag on the greased pole when I stepped out of the elevator and found my way blocked by a nurse's desk and a tired-looking nurse who asked me what in the Lord's name I thought I was doing on her floor at eight o'clock in the morning?

"My grandfather," I said.

"Your grandfather what?"

"The doctor said I could come to see him today. He fell down last Friday and hurt himself. The doctor said . . ."

"You're Mr. Taylor's grandson? I thought he was a bachelor."

"Yes, ma'am. My grandma died a long time before I was born."

"How old are you?" She was tired, but she wasn't too tired to be suspicious.

"Sixteen." The look on her face told me I should have said fourteen, but there was no turning back.

"Don't you know there's such a thing as visiting hours?"

"No, ma'am. I've never been to a hospital before. I just wanted to see my grandfather."

"How come you're not in school?"

"I go to Catholic school, ma'am, and we have a holiday today." If she was Catholic and questioned me, I was cooked.

"Then you can come back at two o'clock this afternoon for regular visiting hours."

"No, ma'am. It's just a half-day so's the teachers can meet in the morning. Please. Can't I see my grandfather now while I'm here?" I thought I was a loser when, unexpectedly, she gave up.

"You might as well, I guess. Look out you don't stay too long. And don't let on that he's still not speaking so good. The doctor says he'll be getting a whole lot better."

He did. A whole lot better. But it took a long time, and for a while he was pretty bad. I couldn't help remembering what that man with the flag had called Derek—a little guy who talks funny—as I stood at the foot of his bed and listened to the garbled noises that came from the mouth of the shrunken man who occupied it. I was so unprepared, what I saw and heard was so shocking, that I almost ran. I had to force myself to shake the big, familiar hand at the end of the scrawny arm that reached out toward me from beneath the bedclothes.

The noises got clearer when Derek filled his mouth with the teeth in the glass on his side table. I had heard about false teeth but I had never seen any before, and I never knew that the big, even white teeth in his smile weren't his. If he spoke to that nurse with his different accent and without his teeth, no wonder she thought he wasn't speaking so good. With his teeth, speaking in an accent that had become familiar to my ears, Derek sounded like a man with a bad stutter or a swollen tongue. In fact his speech improved a lot more than the weakness in his left side which caused him to limp

78

for the rest of his life and to use his right hand for any job that required normal finger strength or dexterity.

Paul's childish laughter on the telephone behind me combined with neighboring children playing on the pavement below to cool my anger and to allow me a slow withdrawal from the flag in his hand. When he had finished his telephone conversation, I would be ready to use reasonable words to tell him how I felt. If only he wouldn't crumple the pitiful remnant of a flag that his hand had once put to better use.

Derek was in the hospital for three weeks and at home for five more before the doctor would let him return to work. During those two months I answered morning roll call at school more often than I had since the fifth grade or would again through my graduation from high school. Not only had the head nurse on Derek's hospital floor warned me not to turn up before regular visiting hours, but I soon discovered that his sister straightened their house in the morning and wanted me to make my daily visits in the afternoon. I ignored her preference only once, the day I received part of a battle flag sent to me by my uncle who was fighting the Japanese in New Guinea.

With the flag he had sent a wonderful letter describing the battle whose shifting fortunes had seen the American jungle headquarters, built several years before by Japanese and hard-won by Americans, overrun again and again—first by Japanese, retaken and lost again by Americans, held for almost a day by Japanese, then finally devastated and taken for the last time, at terrible cost, by an American battalion led by my uncle's company. Because he was the company's top noncommissioned officer, and because all its officers were killed or wounded, he had been offered a battlefield commission and turned it down. When we got to that part of the letter, Derek and I were astounded. Why would he have turned down the opportunity to become an officer? Battlefield commission—what a fine sound those words had. Like red for valor, I said to Derek, and he agreed. Not until long after the war did my uncle tell me that he turned down the commission because he didn't want to worry about the enemy behind as well as the enemy in front. He was sure that two of his officers had died from bullets that had been deliberately fired by American soldiers.

With the flag, in the same letter, came my uncle's usual warning when he sent us forbidden gifts. He was not supposed to send it, we were not supposed to have it, he had only been able to mail it because he was recuperating from his latest and worst attack of malaria in an Australian hospital, and we shouldn't tell anyone about receiving it. His warning, which Derek had no way of knowing was both routine and almost as frequent as his gifts, gave me the reason I needed to leave the flag—actually about a third of the original, but including most of the starred field—on the table in Derek's bedroom. I didn't have to be a friend to see how much he admired it, but he would never have allowed me to leave it if I hadn't convinced him that my uncle's forbidden gift would run less risk of discovery if it were left temporarily with him. It was, his sister said without looking at me as she saw me to the door, a blessed lie and she hoped God would forgive me.

A twenty-four-hour grippe kept me from visiting Derek the day after I gave him the flag for safekeeping. Two days later his sister greeted me at the door, but it was Derek himself, downstairs and sitting in the parlor for the first time, who limped ahead of me upstairs to show me what he had done on the wall of his bedroom. There was my flag re-created in full, the original third comprising the left-hand portion, itself completed by a wall painting done with the utmost accuracy and care. Derek had even lighted it from the side so that the illumination was first caught and softened by cloth, then released to play across the flatter surface of the painted stripes. To my willing eyes the effect was of a battered but whole flag receding from a bright nearness into a darker distance. I was overwhelmed.

"My uncle would like that," I said. It was all I could say, nor did either of us then say more. Later Derek would explain to me how he had stayed up most of the night after I had left the flag with him, stayed up to read his books for information about the proportionate parts of the flag, to measure the dimensions of my remnant and of the retired flag that he kept at home to fly from his bedroom window on holidays, then to

81

draw and paint his projection upon the wall. That
night, I think, marked the real beginning of his recovery from the stroke.

Six days a week for the next four weeks I came to
Derek's house just after lunch and we followed the
doctor's prescription of lengthening walks around
the city. After that first time on the docks, Derek
had asked me no more about school. His sister, however, having no such memory to deter her, wanted
to know how I could come to them so early every
afternoon when other kids didn't seem to get out of
school until two or even three hours later. I explained
to her that I didn't go to public school since my family
was Jewish and Jews went to Jewish schools just the
way Catholics went to Catholic schools. Because I was
afraid she'd question me, I hurried on to the crucial
piece of information: Jewish school began at half past
six in the morning with a religious service, then we
went to class from seven to noon without any play time,
had lunch at school, and were free for the rest of the
day. In a moment of genuine inspiration I added that
Jews were not supposed to work in the afternoon, if
they could help it, just the way they weren't supposed
to work on Saturday, the Sabbath, and that's why we
went to school so early. With that schedule we could be
in school in the morning, play in the afternoon, and do
our homework in the evening. It was a lovely story as
well as a useful invention, and I stepped back to ad-
mire it. Too soon.

"But Derek says you help him with the flag. How can

you help him raise the flag and still be in school so early?"

"Most of the time he only helps me to lower the flag at five o'clock." I was sitting in the parlor with my back to the stairs. I thought Derek was still up in his room, getting ready for our walk.

"There's a lot of Jewish holidays," I said, "and that's when I help Derek raise the flag. On holidays and Saturdays." He had lied to his sister for me and we both knew it.

Our goal was to walk the triangular route that began at Derek's house on Bank Street near Broadway and ran west past the docks to Charles Street, then all the way north on Charles to the Washington Monument, finally completing the triangle with the longest side which extended southeast from the monument mostly by way of Centre Street and High Street back to Bank Street and his house. When he could manage that in one good walk, Derek said, with a rest for my sake at the monument, he would know that the lousy frogs could hurt him but they couldn't do him in. Since the two perpendicular sides of the triangle extended for a total of more than forty blocks while the hypotenuse was at least twenty-five, I had no doubt he would have proved his point if we ever managed to return to his house.

For three weeks we prepared ourselves by walking east instead of west on Bank Street, not toward the waterfront but toward Patterson Park. Each day we increased the distance we traveled, beginning with a six-block round trip and building to the four miles that took us through the park to its eastern edge and back to Bank Street near Broadway. Though Baltimore was having a wet spring, the light rain that fell for some part of almost every day making the new growth of grass in the park greener than I had ever seen, Derek and I never missed a day's walk in four weeks—but for Sundays when I could not come downtown and he walked his prescribed and measured distance by himself. It was almost as though the self-discipline of his rehabilitation were a denial of the wild anger that had left him with a stutter and a limp.

If we talked of many things during the first part of each walk, we always came to the subject of the jungle war in the South Pacific and the flag that now hung on Derek's bedroom wall. He began the conversation one day with his usual question and reassurance: was I sure I didn't want to take the flag home today? After all, he would enjoy finishing the painted flag on his wall, if I took the real portion with me, as much as he had enjoyed measuring and painting the original picture. After I had completed the ritual by reassuring *him* that he was protecting my uncle, my family, and me from discovery by keeping our flag until the war was over, he got to the real subject of our talk.

"Did you know I only went to school three years?" We were sitting on a bench on the far side of Patterson Park, our shoes and socks on the pathway in front of us, drying off a little from our walk through the lush, wet grass.

"You're kidding. Don't they make kids go to school in England?" The hot sun felt good on my wet feet. Only three years. He was making some kind of joke. "Maybe now they do. Didn't then. When I was ten my guv'nor got me a berth as cabin boy on a channel steamer and I never went back to school." Not till years later, living in England, did I discover that the "guv'nor" Derek often referred to was his father.

"Wish I could be that lucky."

"You're a fool!" He spat the words at me with such vehemence that I slid away from him on the bench. Since his stay in the hospital he seemed to be less patient, angrier, less in control of himself. And when he was angry he got harder to understand. But I hadn't misunderstood his tone or his "fool." He was cranking up to say more: "It's going to school that's lucky and you're a fool not to know it. I never knew what I was missing. A cabin boy is nothing. Man with an education—he's something!"

Three years in school for Derek, two for my father. It was always the ones who hadn't done it who thought it was so good to do. I'd have given anything to be a cabin boy, to be able to go to sea and stop wasting my time in school. I was tired of hearing how good school was from people who didn't know anything about it.

"You weren't always a cabin boy."

"If I had done any schooling, I could have had my own ship."

"School stinks. I should know."

85

"How should you know? You don't ever go. And don't tell me about your Jewish school. I wasn't born day before yesterday. That's a lot of John Bull."

The rain was coming again. People on the field below us were walking toward the park shelter. There wasn't any more to say. I started to put on my shoes and socks.

"My sister thinks a lot of you. I went along with your story about Jewish school so she wouldn't worry too much. She's a worrier—about me, about the war, and now about you. We both worry about you, I guess."

The rain was changing from scattered large drops to a thin curtain of wetness in the air, through which the sun was still bright and hot. As we got up from the bench, Derek handed me the brown paper bag with the lunch that I was saving to eat on the other side of the park. We both held it for a moment as he looked directly at me, then out over the playing field toward the shelter as he said, "It's fine of you to come walking with me. You know we'll be tending that flag again. You wait and see if we won't."

We did. On Wednesday, Thursday, Friday, and Saturday of the fourth week we walked the entire sixty-five blocks of the triangle. Wednesday was hardest on both of us, but for different reasons. Because I didn't have a nickel for the trolley car, I had to hitchhike and walk both ways between Derek's house and my own. It wasn't a lucky hitchhiking day, so I mostly walked and ran both ways. In between those two journeys was our sixty-five-block walk. After I finally got home that night, my mother thought I was sick when I fell asleep while eating supper.

For Derek the day was harder, not so much because we had extended our walk from four miles through Patterson Park to some six miles around the heart of the city, but because for the first time in almost two months we would pass *his* flag and *his* flagpole—both in someone else's care. Except to tell me that his job was waiting for him whenever the doctor said he could go back to work, and except for that one reference to tending the flag again when we stood in the warm summer rain at the edge of the park, he had avoided the subject. After several attempts to get him to talk about it, so had I. Because of that, I think, he was somehow unprepared for familiar sights when we walked west toward the docks instead of east toward the park from his home.

Our first stop was at Hilda's lunchroom where the large, kind woman who ran it, who had taken Derek to the hospital and visited him frequently during the two months of his convalescence, greeted us with hot tea, doughnuts, and talk about waterfront people we both knew. Her important news for both of us was the information that several people had been assigned to Derek's work while he was gone but none had done it well. Used to set her clock by Derek, she said; eight and five, the flag up and down that pole every day so you could count on it. Everybody looked forward to having him on the job again. Was it to be next Monday? Not a day too soon.

We stood across the street, freight cars on the tracks of the Baltimore and Ohio dockside railroad looming darkly between us and the slightly moving flag on the great white pole. After the grease had been removed, the pole had been repainted and the slashed lines replaced with new, heavier rope. I had reported all this to Derek in the hospital; now, confronting again the reality of the place that had cost him some part of his speech and his strength, he seemed suddenly too small and too old to have to cope with so much. He sat down heavily on the doorstep of the building behind us. I joined him, the traffic thumping across the cobblestones in front of us making a comfortable, familiar sound in my ears.

"Flag's not tight up to the head." His speech was so slurred that I looked at him out of the corner of my eye to see if he was all right. I could have looked directly into his face and I don't think he would have known. All of his attention was fixed on the flagpole with its drooping flag.

"Pole's dirty, too," I said. "I bet nobody's been washing it the way we did."

"You've got to take care of things or they go all to hell." He spoke slowly, almost to himself, then stared at his hands for a long moment before he pushed himself to his feet and began walking west on Pratt Street, keeping close to the buildings as though he didn't want to be seen in the vicinity of a flag so badly raised and tended. I followed, also keeping to the shadowed part of the sidewalk, not quite knowing why but feeling a vague sense of shame that made me want to avoid the brighter light.

Peace and the Flag of War

An odor, a taste, a sound—all can serve by themselves to recall the shape and texture of a moment so long past that the will to recover it is not enough. Something less subject to voluntary control is needed, something like the flood of emotion released by a child greatly loved crushing lightly in a hand that is flesh of your flesh the flag that is fabric of your past and part of your hope for the future. I was aware that the phone call had ended, that Paul had replaced the receiver in its cradle and was waiting for me to turn my chair from the window to speak with him. The neighboring children no longer played on the sidewalk but I had not seen them go. As I turned to my son, the sidewalk was still populated by other figures, the street in front of our house cobblestones and railroad tracks.

"Why would you want to do that, to sew the flag on the seat of your pants?" He was standing several feet from me, within easy reach, but now it did not matter. The violent moment was past; my question was asked almost without rancor, almost by a spectator at a confrontation between values. I was conscious of time slowing to accommodate us, as though its usual pace were too quick for satisfaction of our needs.

"I don't know. Because that's where it belongs." He spoke from a distance so great that I strained to hear and interpret the words. Why would my son say that the flag *belonged* on the seat of his pants?

"Do what you like. If that's what you have to do, then do it. But if someone knocks you down because he doesn't like it, I won't be there to pick you up. And maybe I'll think you got what was coming to you." I had said it all before I heard the words clearly. I hadn't meant to say it, not in that way. Knock you down. Get what was coming to you. The violence, the same dreadful affliction visited again and again upon the sons of violent fathers. If I couldn't renounce it for myself, why did I have to inflict it upon him?

The violence that reverberated through the room shocked Paul into immobility. He had been my son too long to misunderstand the angry threat, however muted and indirect, of my response. Momentarily frozen before me, eyes wide and lips slightly parted as though caught in the midst of an unspoken word, the hand that held the flag raised itself to his face and, unaware of what it grasped, rubbed slowly across the soft edge of childish cheek and jaw. Had I slapped him, he would have made the same startled, slow, unbelieving gesture.

Only an extraordinary act could have retrieved the moment, could have compounded understanding out of the antagonistic elements that filled the space between us. With a moral force I would not have believed possible in an eleven-year-old child, Paul committed that redeeming act. Half turning from me, his hand still holding the flag against his cheek, he walked the few steps from my desk to the easy chair in my study, sat carefully on its edge, feet together, hands and flag now clutched tightly on his knees, and looked full in my face as he asked, "Why did you say that?"

Tears of pride blurred my vision. I wanted to reach out and take him in my arms, to comfort us both with a gesture of love and protection that would reach deeper than words can go. I did not, for I dared not diminish him or lessen the great stature of his act. Had my father so confronted me, I would have escaped him in anger and hurt confusion. Not six feet from me sat a child full of the bravery and strength I have so long admired in others and wished for myself. My child. Through the veil of my foolish tears I memorized my son's face.

There is an evocative power in gentle certainty that sometimes calls forth truths to match it. For the first time in our life together I was moved to speak to my son of my country, my flag, the immense weight of goodwill and affection that I bore it. I was moved to tell him of his immigrant grandfather who blessed the day my immigrant grandfather had removed his family from medieval Russia to twentieth-century America; of my uncle, his great-uncle, who had died only a few months before on a summer beach after a swim he should never have taken because his heart was so weak from years of fighting against malaria but who preferred death to living like an invalid and who cherished for a quarter of a century the knowledge that he had fought for his country; of a small, bandy-legged Cockney American who knew and loved his adopted country's flag so well that his devotion to it had cost him the clarity of his speech, the strength of his step, and too soon the full length of his life. I told him all this, as best I could, in answer to his question, for all of it was a part of the explanation, a part of the reason why the crumpled flag in his hand and his intention to abuse it had aroused me to such violent denunciation.

And all the time that I spoke, I felt expanded with the pride of his presence.

Was it my joy in America, tempered by the savage fact of the continuing murder in Indochina, that caused him to wait almost a year before he abused the flag? When he made his second decision, he did not come to me to discuss it. Instead, he came to me to announce it, the same small flag now sewn on the back of his blue denim jacket between his shoulder blades.

"Look, Dad," turning his back to me in the doorway of my study, standing where he had stood a year before. It was a careful job of sewing.

"I see."

"I'm going to wear it downtown to the hobby store."

"Good luck."

"I didn't sew it on my pants."

"That's true." I could find nothing more than monosyllables in reply to him.

"I won't be gone long. Do you want to throw the frisbee when I get back?" Conciliatory and decent of him. As he waited for my answer, I realized that I had something to tell him before he went. If I couldn't give him protection, at least I could offer him information.

"Do you know what a super-patriot is?"

"No. Well, maybe. Like somebody who thinks America is always great?"

"That's about it. Sometimes you can tell them by the decals and bumper stickers on their cars. You know—'America: Love It or Leave It' and flags stuck on the windows."

"I saw a dumb one: 'America, Right or Wrong!'

What's that mean? Anything we do is all right?"

"I don't know what it means, but you'll probably get a chance to ask one of them about it."

"Where?"

"Wherever you wear that jacket. It's all right for them to wear the flag on their cars or in their buttonholes, but it's not all right for you to wear it on your jacket. Maybe nothing will happen, but I doubt it."

"I didn't sew it on upside-down and I didn't sew it on my pants. Why should anyone care if I wear it like this on my jacket?"

"Because some people will know that you mean to show disrespect for it and that will make them care a lot." I could hear the argument rising in his throat. "Don't argue with me. Argue with them, unless they're big and angry or there's a lot of them. Then just take it off."

"Nobody can make me if I don't want to."

"Sure they can. I'd think a couple of times before I wore that down on Main Street or on the west side of town. Over here and around the university I don't believe it'll make much difference." I wasn't telling him the truth, at least not all of it, because the truth was that he wasn't entirely safe on the campus either:

It was a hot September day at the end of the first week of classes, with some students still shopping for their semester's courses. Because the early morning had been cool and overcast, I had worn a long-sleeved dress shirt, tie, and jacket which had become more burdensome with the increasing heat of each hour. By

93

the time of my mid-afternoon class I had shed the coat
and tie, but both my superheated top-floor office and
classroom made the shirt intolerable. I was hot, angry
that so many students I hadn't seen before this third
class of the semester had packed themselves into a
classroom far too small to accommodate them all, and
tired after a week of hard work necessary to get the
school year underway. Had I worn a short-sleeved
shirt, had I slept longer the night before, had the day
been cooler and classroom larger. . . . I noticed him
first because he was late, then again because his very
large body filled the aisle where he had at last found a
seat, and finally because he raised one of the biggest,
dirtiest pairs of bare feet I have ever seen to the top
edge of the table in front of him. At that time, late
aisle-sitters with prominent, dirty, bare feet were not
rare enough at Michigan to warrant more than a con-
temptuous glare. But what he may have deserved was
not what he got, the cause having only a little to do with
heat, tiredness, or an overcrowded classroom. It had
much to do, however, with the shirt he wore, a shirt
that bore (beneath its fashionable covering of dirt and
old nourishment) a reproduction of an American flag,
displayed upside-down, with the stars representing
fifty states replaced by fifty small swastikas. Beneath
the flag were two words, "Amerika First."

At the end of the hour he was one of the large group
who came to the lectern to give me their registra-
tion cards for the course. Refusing his—"Hold on to
that," I said. "Come to see me in my office."—I returned there while he and several other students

94

trailed after me. When he entered my office soon after I did, I told him to shut the door behind him in spite of the oppressive heat. When he sat on the chair next to my desk, I could hardly keep my eyes from the flag on his shirt. Nor could I fail to notice that beneath the tight, dirty shirt lay a body that stank.

Suddenly I was red-necked angry with him for his shirt, his feet, his body odor, his existence, and angry with myself for noticing and caring. "Wait here a second," I said abruptly, and went across the hall to the men's room to remove my shirt and wash my face and arms with cold water. I was aware, as I returned to my office wearing my tee shirt, how white it was in contrast to his.

"You don't want to take my class," I said flatly as I sat down again next to him. The water had cooled me a little but it hadn't changed my mind.

"Why not? I like it." He was genuinely startled. In the grip of surprise, forgetting about his face, his mouth fell open. He looked twelve years old, pre-adolescent fat and innocent.

"But I don't like you and it's bound to cost you, no matter how hard I try to ignore it."

"You don't even know me. How can you not like me?" He was amazed. We were both perspiring very heavily.

"You were late and you disrupted the class by climbing over people to find a seat. Then you stuck your dirty bare feet up in my face. I could tell you to get to class on time and keep your feet on the floor, but even if you did it wouldn't make any difference. You're

95

wearing my flag on your shirt and I'd like to make you eat every one of those swastikas. You'd be a whole lot better off in a class where the sight of you didn't make the professor want to knock you on your ass."

My eyes stung with sweat. His shirt was nearly saturated, stains of perspiration spreading from his neck and under his arms down to the top and along the sides of the flag. It appeared to be in danger of drowning. So did he.

"Wow! I can't believe it. I mean I really can't believe it." He was tougher than he looked. His face was already more composed, his eyes watching me carefully. The pre-adolescent was gone, with something more considerable in its place.

"Believe it. We'll both be better off if you do."

"Yeah, I believe it. What are you, a John Bircher or something?"

His words were flat and heavy in the motionless air of the room. I wanted to tell him that I had once prevented a Birch takeover of an educational organization. I imagined speaking the words, and the tone of childish self-righteousness that I heard with them made me cringe. Why should I hide behind the past?

"Something. What are you, somebody with special permission to abuse my flag? If you really knew anything about that swastika, you'd tear that goddam shirt off and burn it."

"I can't believe you. You're not real. You don't exist."

"All right. I tried to warn you. Take the class, then, and find out if I exist. Tell yourself that everybody who'd like to rip that flag off your chest is a Bircher or a hard-hat or some kind of fascist."

"What'll you do if I take your class?" His control was better than mine.

"You won't. The class is listed as 'permission of the instructor' and it's already so far over its maximum number that I don't have to give you permission to register and I won't. You won't be taking it. All I wanted to do is tell you why."

"That's not what you wanted. You wanted to dump on me just the way you think I'm dumping on your flag."

He was right. What I also wanted to do was rip his shirt off and leave a few marks on him when I did it. I had heard myself in the last exchange: Take the class. You can't take the class. I was no more reasonable than he was. Maybe less.

"You're right. But I don't see how that changes anything. I don't want to spend a semester looking at that flag, or seeing your face and thinking about it. *And* I don't have to admit you to my class. Now you tell me. Where do we go from here?"

He slumped slightly in his chair and looked away from me as he spoke. "You know, it's kind of a funny thing. I mean, like it's not even my shirt. I borrowed it from my roommate, but it's not even really his. Some chick just sort of left it in our apartment and it sort of got to be his. Know what I mean? And now it's bringing down all this heavy stuff on me. Heavy, man, and I don't really give a shit. Know what I mean?"

Heavy stuff, heavy silence. Heavy air. I knew what

he meant and I was uncomfortable with the knowledge. "Take the class if you want to. Just do me a favor and don't wear that shirt to class or at least cover it up with something. Come on time and keep your feet on the floor. If you think you can manage to do those things, maybe we can make it through the semester." I had been staring out the window as I spoke, looking toward the graduate library where I could see students sweltering in their tiny study cubicles. When I looked back across my desk, he was on his feet and turning toward the door.

"Not me, man. I mean, you're really some kind of bigot, you know? I don't have it clear in my mind yet, but I get real bad vibes from what you do. You can keep your class. I don't want any part of it."

Swollen with dampness that pervaded everything, my office door stuck in its jamb and refused to open. He stopped tugging at it to dry his perspiring hand on his pants, long enough for me to put words to the question that most troubled me: "Okay. Let's agree to write me off as some kind of bigot who gives off bad vibes. But what about you? Because that's not your shirt, does that mean you're not responsible for the damage it does when you wear it? That swastika belonged to the worst group of murderers in human history and what they did isn't ancient history. It's yesterday, the day before yesterday. Sure Vietnam's so awful that nobody has words to describe it anymore. But comparing America's role in it to Nazi Germany's in the Second World War is like calling the local barn burner Attila the Hun. It's a stupid, vicious form of overkill, and it's a hell of a provocation to bigots like me. Blame everyone else if it makes you feel better, but it's *you* who's wearing that shirt and it's you who doesn't know anything about human history."

I had made a speech on a day that was too hot for breathing, much less speechmaking, but he had heard me out. Now he stood at the door, biting his lower lip, looking as thoughtful as a human being can look when heat and sweat are boiling him alive. Then he moved, slowly, ponderously, away from the door and toward the large wastebasket on the floor beyond my desk. Putting his books down on the edge of the desk, he grasped the bottom of his shirt with both hands and slipped it off over his head by reaching with both hands toward the ceiling. With arms still extended, he moved them through ninety degrees until his outstretched hands held the shirt suspended over the wastebasket. He looked at the shirt for a long moment, then dropped it with a fastidious gesture of his hands. I stood up at my desk and we both stared down into the wastebasket.

"I guess that chickie's never gonna see her shirt again. Wouldn't have fit her now anyway. I sort of stretched it a little out of shape."

I was glad he had said something, for I had nothing at all to say. With his large body jiggling loosely, but strangely dignified for all that, he turned, picked up his books, moved to the door, which he opened with a single strong pull, and left my office without a word or a backward look. Since that time I have seen him on campus and he looks through me as though I don't exist; for him, now, I suppose I don't. But we existed for each other with almost painful intensity on that blazing September day. I'll never lose the sight of him dropping his shirt into the basket and then walking serenely out of my office, sweat glistening on his shoulders and trickling down the small of his back.

John's
Death...

"Do you cry, too, Daddy?"

"Sure. Everybody does, I guess."

"When do you cry?"

"Sometimes late at night, when you and Mother are sleeping."

"I'm crying now because I'm asleep late at night. You could cry now if you want to."

"I guess I don't feel like it now."

"I guess I feel like it." He reached a small hand up to touch his wet cheeks.

"Does John make you feel like it?"

"Yes."

"Me, too."

Paul's brother John was born in March of 1964, a few days after Paul's fourth birthday. The medical practice that was insufficient to bring him to caesarean birth quickly enough after a prolapsed umbilical cord, resulting in severe brain damage from loss of oxygen, was more than sufficient to incubate him over a period of thirty days into a life he did not want to enter. For the nine months of his dying that we had him at home, we all spent a great part of our time holding him or watching him in his crib or playpen, or on a blanket on the floor. The pain of his life—he cried throughout much of each day and night in his anguish from a growing number of small seizures—filled every corner of our home and our lives.

Paul had been sitting next to John's crib, moving the baby's nearly rigid legs as he had seen the physical therapist do when she came to our house. I had come into the bedroom to sit beside him, had discovered tears running down his cheeks as he manipulated John's legs, and had wiped his face with my handkerchief. I could have told him then that I cried often when he and his mother were in the exhausted, fitful sleep that was all any of us knew for almost a year. Though I could have told him that, I didn't. Then and now, I have been beset with the burden of manly propriety: to cry is unmanly enough, but to cry before wife and children is to fail the responsibility of comforter and protector. Fools that we sometimes are, we too often perpetuate our foolishness in our children under the guise of propriety. If I could not accept his invitation to cry with him, I could at least let him know how necessary and how normal his tears were. None of us could afford to keep our grief, unrelieved and unexpressed, to ourselves.

"Will John die, Daddy?" He had stopped moving the unresponsive legs and now sat quietly, his hand still on the baby's bare foot, his face pressed against the bars of the crib, staring at the small, oblivious form of his brother.

"I think so." For the first time, sitting in that room with my two sons, I realized that I wanted one of them to die.

"Do you want him to die?" I was shocked into wakefulness, as though he had heard the words I had barely dared to think.

"Yes, if he has to live like this. I don't want him to suffer any more. If he has to suffer, then I want him to die." The shadows at the head of the bed were darker.

"That's what I want. He's always all bent up like that and crying because it hurts. I want him to die too."

I could see my watch by the night-light on the changing table next to John's bed. One o'clock in the morning and a four-year-old in his pajamas sitting wide awake beside me. The light shone on his flushed cheeks, reflecting from wide eyes that stared at the silent infant in the crib. It was a healing silence that gathered around us, if only for a brief moment. John had cried almost continuously from dinner until just a few minutes past. Without strength to continue, he slept while we watched. Months of listening, watching, waiting had shadowed all our eyes with exhaustion and despair.

John had been born in mid-March and had remained in the hospital until mid-April. Since the house we lived in was made available to us at a very low rent only because its elderly, widowed owner wanted to return from Arizona to occupy it each summer, we had rented a cottage on a lake in northern Michigan from the end of May through the beginning of September. Having been reassured by various doctors that no more in a medical way could be done for John, no matter where he spent his first summer, we drove north at the end of the third week of May with a four-year-old child, a ten-month-old beagle, and a two-month-old infant in the back seat of our old Volkswagen.

For a month of unusually cold weather we spent our days walking through woods and along the lake shore, always carrying at least one and sometimes all three of our companions. Though we could find warmth by walking during the day, we could only find it in the evenings and at night in our unheated cabin by huddling together in front of the fireplace. All of us came intimately to know the dreadful tensions of John's damaged body as we took him from his bed on the coldest nights to sleep warmly among us in our sleeping bags on the stone hearth.

After a summer of blueberries, strawberries, then apples, and through each harvest the unremitting care necessary to keep John alive—there is an astounding will to life in an infant who tries again and again to find his thumb to suck and never succeeds without help in guiding his hand to his mouth; and an equally determined will to give life in a mother who takes six hours a day to feed an infant whose systemic signals will seldom tell him just how to suck or swallow—none of us knew how long we could go on as we were. We had come north resolved that we would learn to care for and to live with John as he was, not as we hoped he would be. Returning south, three and a half months later, we knew how near we had come to discovering the hopelessness of our task.

Now, two months after our return from the north, there could be no more real hope. We had just come from consulting a great neurosurgeon in Chicago who had tested John and told us flatly that medical science did not know how to do what must be done—to suspend the action of his brain so that it could heal instead of destroy itself, so that it could develop alternate pathways while the body survived. He had no doubt that John could not live; when he would die he could not say.

Though what he told us could not have come as a surprise to any observer, and seemed largely to have been anticipated by Martha, I was frightened and deeply shaken. Until the words were irretrievably said, actually loosed by competent authority upon the world, I had been able to hope that the great man with his attendant clutch of young residents would tell us of a new operation, an untested but potentially miraculous drug. . . . He was gone in a flap of white coats, his diagnosis left behind like a cinder blinding the eye of hope. As I watched Martha struggle to dress John's taut body and rigid limbs, I heard Emily Dickinson's line sound and reverberate from the corners of the small, white room. I, too, could not see to see.

Exhausted by all the handling, John slept on my shoulder as we walked through the dilapidated neighborhood that surrounded the hospital, neither one of us able to manage the hard drive back to the apartment where Paul and his grandmother awaited us. After many long blocks had made the death of the child we carried seem less imminent if not less inevitable, we spoke of the hospital and that small, windowless room, of how impossible it must be for that surgeon to repeat similar diagnoses throughout his professional life without protecting himself from the parents' terrible realization and uttermost defeat. The attendant residents, the quick withdrawal, the detached tone of voice—as I forgave him his methods of survival, I thought of Paul and the message we bore him.

"Don't worry about telling Paul," Martha said. Like Paul, she often responds to unspoken thoughts. "Don't worry about saying it. He already knows."

We drove home from Chicago that Sunday evening impelled by an enormous west wind that uprooted trees, barns, and houses in Indiana just south of us and blew our small car at a steady speed beyond its metered maximum along the corridor between Chicago and Detroit. Having no radio, we did not know of the destructive force of the wind; had we known, I do not think we would have cared but for the peril to our sons—and for one, what difference could it make?

The rain accompanying the great wind isolated us within our car, breaking all our ties to the bent and drowning world through which we hurtled. No car overtook us on our way, and only a very few flashed dimly by on the other side of the expressway. When we carried the sleeping children into the house, protecting them from the wind and rain that scoured the night like flung sand, we felt ourselves to be reentering a world of beginnings and ends that too briefly we had managed to escape.

We had returned from Chicago on Sunday night. Only a little more than forty-eight hours later, Paul and I sat beside John's crib and tried to accustom ourselves to the ongoing, certain destruction of the life it contained. His question about John's death was a part of that process, an invitation repeated a dozen times in two days: talk to me so that I can understand. Tell me why this has happened to John and not to me. Tell me why I should have to know so much about death when I don't want to know anything at all. Talk to me. Talk.

He would say to me, only a few years later, that he did not like the television news and the front page of the newspaper because they had so much about killing and death in them. Unlike most other families we knew, we almost never watched the news as it was reported on television, or listened to it on the radio, or read much of the front page of our local newspaper. Paul spoke for the three of us when he told his closest friend, the son of a surgeon, when they were talking about hospitals, doctors, living and dying, that he knew a lot about all those things and didn't have to learn any more.

John died within two months of our return from Chicago. The doctor's prognosis had accomplished the dual effect of weighting us with utter despair and relieving us of the worst effects of hope. Before his pronouncement confirmed what we knew, even if we could not bear to know it, we had been free to search every reflex and gesture for signs of alternate pathways developing in our child's damaged brain. Hope can sometimes make anguish less bearable. As John twisted out of life during that endless autumn, we were at least spared the cruelest experience of watchers who must out-watch hope.

Paul spent a large part of that autumn in John's room, either accompanying his mother during the day or sitting with me at night. At first I was afraid for him, thinking his interest morbid and his frequent presence there unhealthy. Soon I came to understand that he was doing, in the way that fitted him best, exactly what we were doing when we sat our solemn hours beside the crib or playpen. Like us, he had only his presence to offer and he gave of himself what he could. Unlike us, he needed all of those moments of propinquity to separate his fate from that of his brother.

During those countless hours, bereft of hope yet oddly peaceful, watching only because we could not bear that John should go unwatched, watching together because we sometimes could not bear to watch alone, I would talk to Paul of whatever came into my mind in order to ease his passage through the end of his brother's life. Casting about for parallels and likenesses that would let him know he was accompanied in his passage, I told him of the first person loved and lost to death in my own childhood. The name roused him from his somnolence. What, he wanted to know, was a Derek?

I was fifteen, I said, in my first year of high school, when my friend and companion of four years died because we won a war. Though many had died in the war, I told my son, death had not come to the warriors I knew. (Liking the word "warriors," he awakened enough to talk about the "war" that was in it.) Instead, at war's end in September of 1945, my closest friend, who had fought and survived the First World War with only the loss of his teeth, could not endure the joys of victory won thousands of miles away by men young and fit as once he had been. I too had watched at his bedside, as we did now with John, and I too had known that he must die.

But for the weakness in his hand, the limp that had few consequences because he ignored it, and the slurred speech of which he seemed unaware, Derek was a whole man again only a few months after the stroke had felled him. We raised and lowered the flag, washed and whitened the pole, cleaned and trimmed the lines, and we walked. How we walked! I did not understand then, as I do now, that Derek must have attributed the very fact of his existence to the walking program we had pursued together after his illness. If our feet and legs could have bought him freedom from mortality, he would have lived forever.

I smiled inside myself when my father congratu-
lated me for having won the half-mile run on our
junior high school field day. Yes, he said, he had always wanted to be a runner himself and he was glad to
see that I had inherited his speed and his desire. I
smiled because I knew better. If that half-mile run
had depended on speed, I would have been a loser. All
it depended upon was endurance, which by that time I
had more of than I could use. Running a half-mile
around a field was nothing compared to running most
of five miles to get down to the docks in time to raise or
lower the flag, sometimes followed by a sixty-five-
block walk, then the same five miles back home run
and walked as quickly as possible in order not to be late
for supper. Winning a prize for the half-mile run on
field day was like being given an award for breathing. I
had to surpress a feeling of guilt when I accepted the
trophy.

My two greatest discoveries during our walks were
the Catholic cathedral and the Enoch Pratt Free Library. Since Derek was anxious for me to know more
about his Catholicism, having never fully recovered
from my ignorance of George, Andrew, and all other
saints, and proud of his knowledge of his adopted
country's early history, especially of its flag, nothing
was more natural than the deflection one block east of
our customary route north on Charles Street to the
Washington Monument. By walking east one block on
Mulberry, a few blocks short of the monument, we
came to the corner of Cathedral Street where the Free

112

Library and the cathedral faced each other across the intervening thoroughfare.

I could not have known in 1943, when first we stood together at that intersection, any more than I could have know twenty years later when I told Paul about Derek, the cathedral, and the Enoch Pratt as we kept our dark vigil, that I would in the future twice return to that library to give public lectures marking the appearance of two of my books. The child who dozed against me as I spoke of the past, eyelids fluttering against sleep, cheeks puffing slightly with each warm exhalation, was the same child who would sit in my second audience at the Pratt, eight years later, and smile tolerantly as I told stories of schoolchildren, himself included. Next to him his mother and sister, throughout the audience beloved family and old friends—of all who should have been there, only Derek absent, in whose company I had first made my cautious way into the library through the Cathedral Street doors. When the lecture was done and all gone but family and friends, I took my son by the hand and led him to the window that I might show him the corner of Mulberry and Cathedral. No bandy-legged little man stood among the impatient crowds. Dispossessed of the past, I held tightly to the hand that held the future.

During the winter before the war ended, after three years of unremitting and unsuccessful effort, I finally convinced an adult male that I was eighteen years old. Unhappily, that adult male was not a recruiting officer for any of the armed services of the United States. To the end of the war they persisted in believing me too young to fight for my country. The man I convinced was the owner of a Maryland summer camp for boys and girls from six to sixteen. Perhaps he believed me because he had to. Warm male civilian bodies, eighteen years or older, were in very short supply in the summer of '45.

In the previous summer I had found a job as clerk in a downtown pawnshop about eight blocks from the waterfront, where I had been able to join Derek morning and evening six days a week for two months to raise and lower the flag, and at noon to have a walk around the city. But the job was dull, the city hot, and during the next winter I discovered I knew a boy who knew a boy who knew a man who was looking for someone to teach swimming and riflery at his summer camp. After convincing myself that I could teach both, I convinced him that I had, spoke carefully during the interview to keep my unreliable voice from fluctuating between tenor and bass, got a friend to sign his stepbrother's well-known athletic name to a laudatory letter typed on his well-known athletic letterhead, and got the job. Derek said he was happy for me, and I think he was. He must have recognized what I myself did not know or did not want to know: more than two years of walks and four years of flag-raising had left me with the need for other people and other experiences. What neither of us knew was that we would be apart during the last summer of his life.

When Japan's surrender was announced over the radio early in August, my friend who signed his brother's name to letters put our contingency plan into effect. A phone call to the camp director said that my grandfather had been overcome with the excitement of the news, had collapsed on the street, and might not survive twenty-four hours. I should come home if I wanted to see him alive. With much kindness and sympathy, the director himself took me to the nearby village and advanced me money against my summer's salary, payable at the end of the season, for the round-trip bus ticket and five dollars besides. My conscience turned. Had I thought he would have understood how important it was to raise the flag with Derek on the day of victory, I would have told him the truth.

Those were two of the most wonderful days of my life. Because my family thought I was at camp, and because Derek was so delighted to see me—I had told him I would come if Japan surrendered during the summer, but he was surprised at my appearance—I stayed at his house for the first time. Though I stayed there, I did not sleep there; in fact, neither one of us slept much anywhere in spite of blankets and pillows we carried from Derek's house to the flagpole. Both nights were taken up with tending the great secret we had hoarded throughout the latter part of the war: a large GI searchlight with extra batteries and bulbs, all liberated by Derek from a truck smash-up that had taken place in the docks area. He wouldn't have taken it for himself, he said, but our flag would deserve it when the war finally came to an end.

Both of us knew every important provision of the Flag Code which became Public Law 829 when the Seventy-seventh Congress adopted the Code as law in 1942. The Flag Code had been around for a long time before that, maybe twenty years Derek said, but it wasn't until we went to war that Congress decided to adopt it as the law of the land. I got to see it for the first time at the Enoch Pratt, where Derek went to check his old copy of the Code against the new law. What he wanted to be sure of, he said, was that our scheme for using the liberated searchlight was legal, more or less.

We found the confirmation we sought in the Code's provision for special occasions. Federal law would allow us to display the flag at night out-of-doors, which solved our biggest problem. What local authorities would have to say about our searchlight was a question we decided to ignore. Neither one of us thought for a moment on V-J Day of the possibility that our country could still be at war even after having won a war, that Japan would not surrender unconditionally until September and therefore civil defense blackout rules would still be officially in force. For a few wild, wonderful hours, the war in the Pacific didn't exist.

But only for a few hours. Our searchlight had severe and nearly fatal problems which required our constant attention. We soon discovered that it was no simple matter to keep the flag illuminated for the celebration that resounded behind us in the city. Though the bulbs fit the searchlight, they seemed unable to accommodate the full power of the batteries. After a warning flare of extra brightness, they were gone. Since our supply was finite, though large, and the night lay limit-lessly before us, we were caught up in by-passing bat-teries and juggling bulbs when the cop on the horse swept down on us from the city.

"Derek!"

The voice came out of the night air behind and above us. Without a fifteen-year-old heart and ner-vous system to match, I would have died from shock. I hadn't heard the horse on the cobblestones; I hadn't heard anything but the sizzling of the rag I used to protect my hand from the overheated bulb I was trying to loosen in its socket. Then, suddenly, that voice and the snorting of an animal behind me. I was frozen in a permanent squat next to the searchlight. I couldn't have gotten up or turned around if my life had de-pended on it.

"Derek! What the hell is going on here?"

Did he think I was Derek? My tongue was so big and dry in my mouth that I couldn't have told him my name if he'd asked me. Derek's voice came out of the blackness beyond the light.

"What's up, Timothy? You gave us a start, coming down on us so sudden like."

"Man, it's you who gave me the start! What in God's holy name are you trying to do with that light? Make the Jap's work easy? Shall it be Pearl Harbor in '41 and Baltimore Harbor in '45? Do you not know we're still at war?" I liked the way his voice sang the words, but I didn't like the nearness of that horse's head. When he rode slowly around the light toward Derek's voice, I sank backward onto the curb, sucked my burned fingers, and awaited my fate. No use trying to out-run a horse.

Derek was standing next to the horse's stirrup, his hand on the harness, talking so softly that I couldn't make out the words. The bulb that I hadn't managed to loosen was flaring again; soon it would go out, and the flag would be left to fly in darkness. The harbor breeze was soft, moving the flag gently away from the water and north toward the noisy city. I was lost in watching it when a familiar voice asked me if I thought we had all the bulbs in the world and some to spare?

"Derek!"

"Who'd you expect? Jungle Jim?"

"Where's the cop?" I strained my dazzled eyes to see past the light.

"On his horse, both going about their business as every man should on so grand a night." He was imitating Timothy the cop. As he spoke, he pointed west on Pratt Street. Following the line of his finger, I saw the horse's rear end moving slowly down the center of the street. Find a horse's ass, find a cop, my uncle always said. I decided Timothy must be in the darkness above the departing horse.

"I was scared he'd ask me how old I am. I never even thought about the downtown curfew."

"Not to worry. It's a very special night."

"But we've got to cut off the light. The cop said . . ."

"What he said and what he said were two very different things."

118

"You mean we don't have to blackout the light?" I was incredulous. If the cop said we were still at war, we were still at war. That meant no lights showing at night. I stared up at Derek's smiling face, then followed his arm as it pointed once more, this time not at the retreating horse but up into the air, toward the night sky behind me.

"Look there, lad. Use the eyes the good Lord gave you and look just there." He was still imitating Timothy, having his fun at a time that was anything but funny. Again I followed the line of his finger, this time pointing north into the sky above the city. I saw nothing and said so, angry at his play-acting.

"Then look again, boy, because you're sand-blind from staring too long at the searchlight. Now look again."

I looked. And then I gawked like a country boy in the city, Derek told his sister next morning at breakfast. I gawked because I was shocked, astounded, unable to comprehend what I saw, feeling as primitive man must have felt the first time he faced fire: the downtown sky was ablaze with light. On the streets where the crowds surged, sounding their bells and whistles and drums, their noisemakers, horns, and guns, giant searchlights made mad patterns in the sky above buildings that must have had every bulb ablaze in order to account for the brightness of the air. For three and a half years no eyes in America had seen such a sight.

Like me, Timothy the cop had been so taken up with his work that he had forgotten the world around him.

119

When Derek had invited him to look at the sky over downtown streets, Timothy had thought him frivolous; again like me, he had at first seen nothing. Even when his mind had grasped what his eyes were viewing, he had begun to argue that downtown and harbor were not the same, that . . . Derek had laughed him into defeat. Our flag was illuminated for all of two nights except for those moments when we changed bulbs and replaced batteries. No one mentioned blackout or curfew again.

I went back to camp to a chorus of sympathy for my grandfather who, miraculously, now seemed likely to survive the excitement of victory. If Japan formally surrendered before the camp season was over, Derek and I had agreed that he could get along without me as he would illuminate the flag for only part of one night. Nevertheless I stopped at my cousin's house, who was also my banker for pool and cards, to pick up a small part of my bankroll in case I had to make the trip again. I didn't think my grandfather's health was elastic enough to cover the full requirements of two emergencies.

My grandfather survived both victory celebrations and some years thereafter, but Derek did not. He had his second stroke on the morning of 3 September 1945 and died in the hospital one week later as his sister and I were leaving his room to take our brown bag lunches to the hospital cafeteria. He had been dying for a week, retreating further and further from the stimuli of our voices and various medical attempts to evoke response. The week had begun when his sister discovered him on the floor next to his bed late in the morning of the day after MacArthur accepted Japan's surrender aboard the battleship *Missouri* in Tokyo Bay. He and I had worked together until midnight illuminating the flag at the apparent cost of burned fingers and dazzled eyes. But the real cost to Derek was his life, which he gave up with a small sound that caused us to turn in the doorway of the hospital room to look back at him. We both knew then that he was too quiet to be alive.

Because Paul was now sound asleep against me, I did not continue my story. Had he been awake I would have found some other story to tell than the tale of intended honor which, for me, was not honor but horror, horror beyond belief and beyond comparison until I sat beside the crib of my son not yet dead. The honor had been done me by Derek's sister, who asked if I would like to sit with her beside Derek's coffin while friends came to pay their last respects. How was I to know that I was to sit beside an open coffin for nearly a whole day and evening, looking at the face of my friend who no longer looked like my friend but like a ravaged wax dummy never possessed of life? Twice in the morning the horror of it was more than I could bear, both times forced upon me by his sister's tearful, prideful question, "Doesn't he look like himself? So relaxed and natural." He looked like no one I had ever known or seen, nothing that had ever lived upon Earth. Twice I retreated through the flowers and down the carpeted aisle to the men's room where I locked myself in a stall and cried for Derek and for me.

Paul and John and Derek and I came together once more during the autumn that we awaited John's death. Paul and I had taken Arfie, our beagle, for exercise in the university Arboretum and we had gone farther than our walks usually allowed. On an unfamiliar upland trail, Arfie had snuffed a heavy scent and rushed away from us into a nearby patch of woods. We followed, unconcerned at the beagle's distancing sound until we broke through the trees onto clear ground and discovered that a high fence which separated the Arboretum from an adjacent cemetery also separated us from our dog. After locating the break through which he had gone, we followed him among the tombstones.

By the time we found Arfie we were so far from our point of entry that it was easier for us to continue through the large cemetery to its entrance than to retrace our steps. We walked slowly, regaining our breath after a long run, and I became aware that my companion was holding very tightly to my hand.

"Where are all the dead people?" Abruptly asked, the question was preceded by a sudden halt in our progress. Though the question was asked of me, it was not directed toward me. Still holding my hand, Paul had leaned forward to read a small tombstone at the edge of the cemetery roadway on which we stood. I too leaned over to read and saw the single name carved on the stone.

"There're a lot of people named Paul in the world."

"That's not me."

"Of course it's not. You're here and you're alive.

He's there, and he's dead."

"What's his last name?"

We walked through the ring of small stones to the central monument with the family name upon it. Paul traced it out with his finger, then repeated his question. As he asked me again where the dead people were, I realized that he had never been in a cemetery before.

"In boxes in the ground."

"Down there?" pointing with his finger at the earth beneath our feet.

"Down there."

"We're walking on top of them?"

"There's six feet of earth between us and them. Besides they don't care. They're dead."

"Like John's going to be."

"Just like."

One hand holding to his father's hand, the other holding to his dog's leash, he walked beside me in silence. His next question, when it came, didn't surprise me as much as the first. I had been thinking about it a good deal myself.

"Are we going to put John in a box when he's dead?"

"No, I don't think so. Your mother and I don't like the idea of filling up the earth with bodies. We'll probably have him cremated." Until I said it, I hadn't been sure I wanted to do it. As I said it, in that place, I knew why: none of the names on any of the stones, whether ancient or recent, was Derek, though we found numerous Marthas and Johns and Daniels and Pauls, yet he was all too present on the long, slow walk, present not in his own vital flesh but in the monstrous, dehumanized waxiness of his coffined self. I could not let that be done to my son.

I explained about the great heat that would reduce a body to ashes that could then be scattered upon the earth from which they came. Even though we walked in a cemetery, pitiful remnants of life interred beneath us, a cold wind blew the sky clear above us and I could not help but think that we had begun to win through. Dog on leash, father and son walking slowly, speaking soberly, we had managed to incorporate the end of life into living itself. When we reached the cemetery gates, we increased our pace and started to walk briskly toward home.

Paul's profound participation in his brother's life and death has combined with his personal knowledge of insanity in one of his cousins to create in him a kind of broad fatalism which is often misunderstood as apathy when found in older adolescents or young men and women of college age. In spite of the previous generation's apparent commitment to the righteous anger born at Berkeley, nurtured at Columbia and Chicago, and buried at Kent State, the commitment was narrowly based in a small fraction of the generation and the anger was never far from despair. What is now succeeding the anger and replacing the despair, I think, is an intelligent recognition of what does not matter and an intense, motivating disgust at the wrongness of what must be changed. Only the uncivilized define quietness as apathy; only the morally dull could equate apathy with the quiet determination of most of the young men whose moral disgust caused them to abandon their birthright rather than fight an unjust war.

I have watched Paul grapple with the facts of death and madness, I have watched him find a subordinate place for them in his scheme of things, and I have drawn strength from his strength when my own supply was exhausted. Until I discovered what a source of renewal the strength of a child can be, I had thought the flow of dependence ran entirely the other way. Though I realize now that I drew upon my son's strength long before I was aware of doing so, I remember clearly the moment of discovery.

Paul had a school holiday on a day I did not teach and could remain at home while Martha took Lisa to nursery school and spent the morning at the university. A troubled friend from the neighborhood, a nine-year-old child of great capacities and great strains whom we had seen through a recent crisis of compulsive thievery, had come to spend the morning with Paul and Kenny, our fourteen-year-old nephew. Kenny was visiting us on leave from the hospital school where he lived, his precarious grip on reality shattered seven years before by the death of his mother, Martha's sister, in childbirth. Within the year of her death, Kenny had been institutionalized as schizophrenic. This visit with us, which eventually encompassed six weeks, was the first time since the year of his original commitment that he had been out of the institution for more than seven days together.

We talked for a confused and worried year before

we brought Kenny to us for a stay of purposefully indeterminate length. We had sought advice everywhere, and everywhere it had ranged from predictions that were neutral at best to starkly negative at worst: "We tried it, with children we couldn't resist, a couple of times when we were your age and a couple of times when our kids were older," warned a good friend whose work as a children's psychologist is widely known. "Each time we had to give up because of the child's effect on us."

"How about your children?" I asked, for Kenny's effect upon our children was our chief concern. What was there to fear for ourselves?

"Don't worry about your children. Worry about yourselves. Children can accommodate to insanity in ways you can't even learn from, much less duplicate. It's your own stability that will be threatened, not your children's."

Having been warned, we refused to listen. Looking back, after the first experience, we understood that it was something we had to do. Once assured that neither our four-year-old daughter nor nine-year-old son had anything to fear from this gentle, tragic boy, we could not afford to heed warnings about the effect upon ourselves. Even Kenny's desperate need may have been less important than our need to help him if we could.

Because on that day I could not work with the sound of Kenny's keening rising from the living room above the muted music of the radio he kept pressed to his head, and because I felt unequal to taking him on one

of the long neighborhood walks that was the rarest of
joys to his confined spirit, I stared at a wall of books
and listened aimlessly to the sounds of the house. In a
room down the hallway from my study, Paul and his
friend were watching television, playing with battery-
powered cars on a floor full of orange-colored plastic
track, and arguing about the effects of great fear.

"Suppose you're really afraid," his friend replied to
something Paul said. "So what can you get?"

"You can get crazy or dead," Paul answered, speaking with such emphasis that each word seemed to burst
upon the next. "Kenny's afraid all the time. That's
what makes him crazy."

"Will he hurt you?"

"Who? Kenny?" Superior in his knowledge, Paul
laughed at his friend's fear. "No. He's nice. He's just
crazy."

You can get crazy or dead. I wrote his words inside the
front cover of a paperbound text of Shakespeare's
King Lear that I was preparing for class. I have the text
in front of me; the intervening distance of time to
forget now lets me see what escaped me when I wrote
the words: how appropriate they are to the theme of
that play. Four years ago, when I overheard the words
in Paul's mouth, I could think only that they were the
apt distillation of his own experience.

In spite of our friend's warning, it was Lisa and Paul
who taught us how to live with Kenny. For Lisa, he was
an inexplicably large four-year-old who liked to do
many of the things she did, so they did them together
or in parallel. For Paul, who knew most of what we

knew and understood some of it, he was a problem to be dealt with as Paul deals with many of his problems—openly, and in this case with devastating directness.

One of Kenny's many obsessive anxieties was the weather in all of its manifestations but especially in the form of wind, rain, and thunderstorms. Nothing made him more apprehensive than a rising wind, and nothing frightened him more deeply than a thunderstorm. He spent a good part of his day listening to weather reports on his small transistor radio, as well as peering out doors and windows to discover what nature might threaten.

At breakfast one bright, clear Saturday morning in November we had pressed Kenny to tell us about the hospital school in northern New York State where he lived. Though we had pressed very gently, we had been persistent because we saw it only briefly and selectively, and we knew we were exposed to its cosmetic face. What was it really like, we wanted to know, and how were the children treated?

For Kenny, who had been with us for several weeks and was already inventing pitiful little stratagems to ensure his return ("I'll leave my radio [his most precious possession] here so I can get it next time."), our questions must have been intolerably evocative and threatening. When breakfast was done, he rose from the table into a cloud of insanity that darkened the sun and desperately untuned our Saturday morning household. The climax of his frightening regression came late in the morning when he ran to the living room window and pronounced, in a great voice broken with terror, a huge thunderstorm on its way to Ann Arbor.

Paul, who had been lying on the floor listening to a record, leaped up and ran to look out the window through which Kenny stared. Seeing the same cloudless sky above the still tops of autumn trees, he turned to his cousin and said loudly, above the noise of the phonograph, "Kenny, that's crazy. There aren't any clouds and there isn't any wind and anyway thunderstorms don't happen now. They happen when it's warm. That's really a crazy thing to say." And with that he turned his back and returned to his comfortable position on the floor.

I was dumbstruck. My heart was pounding so heavily that even the sound of the phonograph was blurred and dim. *Crazy!* He had actually used that word twice, word of all words most forbidden, most fatal to our hopes of helping Kenny, most. . . . Kenny watched Paul return to listening, looked again out the window at the bright sky, shook his head and said loudly, "Yep. That's really crazy." With which he joined Paul on the floor and I lay back on the sofa to rest my fears.

The long neighborhood walks, walks in the countryside, walks through the university Arboretum—just as they were Kenny's greatest joy, they were also one of his most severe trials. The child of tall parents, he was already exceptionally long and wiry at fourteen and would grow enormously between his subsequent yearly visits. Even when he reached six feet and more, however, he was still subject to the phenomenon that

Paul identified as "shrinking" when we all noticed it repeatedly during his first visit to us. It remains one of the most disturbing physical manifestations of mental illness I have ever seen.

Kenny was always expansive as we prepared for a walk. It was he who would check to see that his younger cousins were properly dressed, the back door locked and the dog on leash. His expansiveness lasted until the front door closed, until we descended the flight of steps from our porch, or perhaps until we left the car if we were not taking a neighborhood walk. No matter how buoyant his enthusiasm, no matter how clear and windless the day, his expansiveness never lasted beyond visual contact with the first person or group of people we would have to pass. That we might know them and greet or be greeted by them made no difference. As Paul said, Kenny actually seemed to get smaller, reduced before our eyes as the weight of human creatures pressed upon him. Within a block he would be so bent and compressed that merely to look at him was to feel the pain of his existence.

If the walk were long enough, Kenny would have grown again close to his normal size by the time it was done. But that was very long to wait if he was in your eye during the entire period of shrinking and expanding. It was Paul, troubled as we all were by this manifestation of his cousin's tortured retreat from the world, who found a remedy. We had just left our car parked around the corner from the entrance and were standing at the top of the Arboretum hill that falls toward the Huron River. A group of laughing adolescents was

130

climbing up from the river valley toward us, their happiness reflected in voices that traveled before them up the brown slope. We all paused to watch them; even the beagle was momentarily more attentive to the quality of the sound than to his desire to be freed from the leash's restraint. I believed the others were equally engaged with the sounds and colors of the day until my belief was shattered by Paul's voice pitched almost hysterically high against the deep rumble of a truck passing on the avenue behind us.

"Kenny! Come on! Let's run with Arfie!"

I saw him slip the leash from the dog's collar, push his much larger cousin in front of him, then race around him after our rapidly departing hound. Kenny stumbled slightly, looked back at me for a moment with such a curious, baffled pleading in his eyes, his face contorted with uncertainty and desire, that I swept my arm outward from my body in the same gesture I used to tell the dog he was free to run, and Kenny began to unwind like an upright serpent down the Arboretum slope. As he ran, he grew; when he passed from our sight, he might almost have been any fourteen-year-old boy somewhat unaccustomed to running after departing dogs and children. I stared into the mouth of the pathway where he had vanished, willing him to grow, to attain his full stature in the race to the river.

Ten minutes later, full of trepidation that had increased with each section of pathway that revealed itself empty as Lisa and I made our slow way down to the valley, I was shocked to discover Paul sitting by

131

himself against a tree watching a few undergraduates play touch-football. No Kenny, no dog. I nearly panicked. The boy almost certainly hadn't been outside by himself, unless on his institution's school playground or on our front porch, in seven years. My mind tried to block the rush of disaster as it coursed through the trees and pathways of the Arboretum.

"Kenny . . ." I said, and got no further, my worst fears realized in the tears on Paul's flushed cheeks.

"Ran away from me," Paul managed to get out between tearful gulps. "Arfie knows I can't run as fast as he can and Kenny's legs are *this* long." His woeful face and arms, outstretched to show the length of Kenny's legs, were momentarily too much for my sense of disaster. My laughter brought fresh tears to his eyes and an angry protest to his lips:

"I did it for him and he can't even wait up for me. He's a rat!"

Arfie? No, Kenny. Both? "Who did you do what for? Who's a rat?"

"Kenny. He looked so all shrinked up when we stood on the hill that I wanted him to take Arfie and run. I don't like it when dumb people stare at him like he was a freak or something." Even very understanding people would sometimes stare at Kenny for a moment before kindness diverted their attention. Twisted and compressed into a hard knot of anguish, he could not be entirely ignored even by the most sensitive passerby.

"Where did they go?"

"How should I know?" More tears. "They wouldn't wait up for me."

Snuffling beside me as well as in front of me; Paul's tears were making Lisa cry. Two crying children, Kenny and Arfie lost—my God! the sound that was trying to intrude itself between sobs from both children was Arfie baying on the trail of some creature. The sound ceased, began again on a new note, and I knew his quarry had been treed or gone to ground. Carrying one child, nearly dragging the other, I raced toward the sound. All I could see was a nightmare vision of Kenny crouched like an animal at bay in the branches of a tree, or huddled in the back of a burrow. Then I heard another sound that caused me to drop Paul's hand and really run for it.

Kenny's laugh was of a piece with the rest of him —distinctive, abnormal, disquieting. It was his wild, high laughter I heard interspersed with the dog's baying that sent me racing down into the valley with Lisa in my arms, Paul outdistanced and left behind for the second time in ten minutes. As I ran toward the sound it seemed to recede from me and I thought of the phantom hunters with their faithful dogs who, having hunted forbidden game, were said to be doomed eternally to course the forests of the world. What sort of phantom tempted me over the hillocks and through each copse?

Whatever had gone to ground in the hole into which Arfie bellowed while Kenny danced about behind him, laughing and clapping his hands, would be unlikely to

133

emerge for the rest of its life, if it had not already died
of fright in the depths of its burrow. Nothing quite like
Arfie's and Kenny's commingled sound could have
ever been heard in the world before, by human or
creature ears.

"Uncle Dan! Uncle Dan! Listen to Arfie! He's got a
toad in his hole. Yep. A toad!"

I looked at the burrow mouth as I snapped the leash
on Arfie's collar. A toad? It would have to be the
world's biggest. . . . Kenny was laughing again, and
I realized he was making a joke. Arfie licking Lisa's
face as she sat crying on the ground at my feet, Paul
plodding up on his short legs to take the leash from my
hand, Kenny filling my mind's eye as I realized what I
was seeing. He was upright, absolutely upright. Un-
bent, unknotted, unafraid . . . he took the leash
from Paul's hand before either one of us could protest
and walked ahead with independence and dignity,
leading us back through leaf-filled woods to the brown
slope that rose to the entrance and our car. Though
we passed a number of people on the way, not one
looked at him with more curiosity than any person
gives to a boy walking a dog anywhere in the world.

"Nobody's looking at him," Paul said, putting the
same thought into words.

"No reason for it. He looks fine."

He did. It was astounding, but he looked almost
normal as we walked slowly back up the hill. He had
been trusted to be alone and to care for another creature, and in his own way he had managed to repay both
trusts, however reluctantly given. For every one of the

many walks together we have taken in ensuing years, Kenny has taken Arfie himself; wherever appropriate, he has released the dog and run with him. No matter how bent and shrunken he may be when the walk or run begins, he is more upright and expanded when it ends. Paul, whose memory of being left behind has receded as his legs have lengthened, sometimes runs with them but more often does not. Understanding Kenny's need to do it himself, he is proud of the apparent change in him, glad that passersby have less reason now to gape, and especially pleased that putting his dog and his cousin together was his idea. For him, I think, Kenny has been a means to discovering the pleasures of unbidden kindness.

Four episodes in Paul's relationship to Kenny brought me information about my son that increased his stature in my eyes. First was the directness of language and action in a child old enough to choose deviousness if it had fitted him; second, and far more important, was the complex fabric of our experience in the Arboretum; third was our first visit together to the institution in New York State where Kenny had been confined since his seventh birthday; and last was his treatment of his cousin after Kenny had been released from the institution of his confinement into his grandmother's care. Of the four, the third was most difficult because it was the only one that was not a spontaneous meeting of an immediate need.

Having taken the opportunity arising from several lectures in the area, I was the first of our family to visit Kenny after his initial commitment. I had dreaded the experience, my imagination building and destroying monstrosities of every sort as I drove from the airport toward the institution. Oddly, perhaps, it was not the prospect of insane human beings that frightened me; instead, it was the state hospital itself that tightened my stomach and made my hands damp on the steering wheel. I had known damaged children and adults all my life—immigrant neighborhoods used to be full of the defective and deranged; no matter how unwise, old-country families usually refused to give up their own—but I had only known a single mental hospital and that had been medieval in its dreadful confinement. I did not expect to find that, and yet. . . . The grounds were beautiful but some of the windows were barred. The cheerful young man at the desk said that Kenny had been expecting me for a week even though he knew I would not arrive until today. I stood while they fetched him. I was too ill-at-ease to sit.

Suddenly he was there, enormous brown eyes in a face so thin that he looked all the more like girlhood pictures of his mother. Tall but bent, nervous, unable to stop smiling or saying my name, he wanted to be embraced, to be held and petted and not to talk. We sat for an hour on the sofa in the small waiting room, my arms around him, his head against my shoulder, hospital life moving quietly about us, leaving us out of time in the isolation of his need. That hour, the long day together that followed, the man with his attendant whom we passed while we walked hand-in-hand through the hospital grounds—all combined to convince me of the mistaken decision I had made about Kenny and my family.

After our hour together on the sofa, we spent the rest of the morning playing on the playground next to Kenny's building and shopping for small items from the well-stocked commissary in the main building. They didn't have what he *really* wanted, Kenny pointed out as we left with a large bag of candy, games, and toilet articles, but anyway he liked everything he'd got. When I asked, as I was supposed to, what that might be, his sweet smile thanked me for allowing myself to be manipulated into being told that he *really* wanted a frisbee because one of the boys in his dormitory had one and the nearest place they could be bought was in a town some ten miles away. And he sure wished he could go into that town this afternoon and get one.

We got two. Because Kenny was unable to decide between blue and white, we avoided a difficult decision by taking both. Three hours, one lunch, one very long window-shopping walk, and two banana splits later, we were back on the institution's grounds throwing both frisbees back and forth to each other. When I pleaded exhaustion and sat in the lush grass against an old oak, Kenny threw the frisbees at various targets. It was then that I saw the little man who looked so much like the Samuel I used to know. I stared at him across the park as he shuffled down the roadway.

The resemblance was near enough at a distance to be startling. When he and his attendant stopped at a bench across the lawn from us, I willed them to come nearer but it appeared they were preparing for a long sit in the sun. I had to see that little man more closely. Holding hands, each of us carrying a frisbee, Kenny and I took a route that would lead us behind their bench. I hadn't thought of Samuel in twenty years:

She was Samuel's mother, aunt, sister, or nurse. I think she told me which, but it didn't matter because I wasn't paying attention to her. I was scared witless by the creature who stood beside her, who had approached unseen behind me while I was throwing my ball against the garage wall and had grunted in my ear. A little grunt would have been more than enough, but Samuel's specialty was a very big grunt delivered as close to the ear as possible. In this case it couldn't have been any closer or much louder. I don't know how far I jumped, but I had climbed the drain pipe to the garage roof before I knew I hadn't been threatened by a wild animal. Small and squat, with long arms and a bullet head, the creature that had frightened me stood next to the spot I had just abandoned and grunted disconsolately to itself.

We had moved into the neighborhood only a few weeks before. One of the boys in the apartment block across the alley behind us had told me that a crazy lived in the corner house on my street and I should watch out for him. I didn't know exactly what a crazy was, but I watched the corner house carefully since it was clearly something to be wary of. After several weeks, when nothing happened and I had heard the boy who gave me the information referred to as "mountain trash," I decided that he had just been trying to scare me and I began to play down at that end of the block. Finally I got so bold that I took to bouncing my ball against the wall of the garage that belonged to the house where the crazy was supposed to live and obviously didn't. It took only a single grunt to convince me that I'd been wrong and the boy had been right. From the safety of the garage roof I looked down on Samuel and his companion and I knew what a crazy was.

The neighborhood myth was that Samuel was harmless, but that was the necessary myth we used to protect ourselves from all the damaged human creatures who sat endlessly on their porches or wandered our neighborhood with or without their keepers. The fact is that some were perfectly harmless and some were purely dangerous, and most fell somewhere in between. Like Samuel, who was surprisingly strong as well as quick enough to hurt you with the broom he often carried, and who did not like to be baited or mocked. After I saw him catch one of the nastier neighborhood kids and hit him across the calves of his legs with a broom handle, I decided that it was safer to be his friend than his enemy.

As much as Samuel could be anybody's friend—I was told that he was a "Mongolian" and had the intelligence of a three-year-old child—he was mine. After several years of being nice to him, which meant playing ball with him occasionally and greeting him whenever he came outside to watch us skate in the street, I was given the Saturday morning job of accompanying him two blocks to the local barbershop where he received his daily shave and weekly haircut. For some reason, perhaps the fact that on Saturday morning the neighborhood was full of kids who were in school from Monday through Friday, Samuel wasn't trusted to go by himself on Saturday as he was on the other days of the week. For a nickel, sometimes a dime, and once, magnificently, a quarter, I was Samuel's Saturday morning companion.

In the spring of my tenth year, a few months before we moved from Samuel's neighborhood, I earned the only quarter I ever had to spend without accountability before I was thirteen. It was given to me by the woman who was Samuel's keeper as a reward for hitting Samuel with a rock hard enough to break his head and make him nearly unconscious.

We had to cross two streets to get to the barbershop. For the first few Saturday mornings that I had the job, we took the alley passage between the two streets because, as I told Samuel when he grunted unhappily at the change in his normal route, it was shorter than staying on the connecting avenue. The truth is that it wasn't shorter at all, and both of us knew it. We took the alley instead of the street because I liked Samuel's money but I was ashamed of his company. And I was afraid of what might happen if the rough boys on the intervening block saw us together. In the narrow alley I could walk far enough behind or in front of him so that I could always disclaim being his companion if that were necessary. On the broad street, however, that was impossible, exposed as we were to everybody's eyes for the entire length of our two-block walk.

If I hadn't already spent the money in my imagination for a movie that afternoon, I think I would have quit my job on the Saturday morning that I called for Samuel and the woman told me to keep to the streets and out of the alleys. Samuel didn't like alleys, she said, and my job was to walk with him on his normal route to the barbershop. That's what I was being paid for, and that's what I was expected to do.

As we began our walk, I concentrated on the nickel I would get and the movie I would see. My mother would give me two cents for candy and I would have a fine afternoon. The thought carried me through the first block, which was mine and unlikely to bring trouble, across the first street and into the second block which was unlikely to bring anything but trouble. Halfway up the block, the two boys who worried me most were playing stepball against two strangers. With no way to avoid them, since their game used both sidewalk and street, we would have to pass right through the middle of their play. Oblivious, happy in the new spring warmth, Samuel grunted and shambled along beside me.

They had seen us coming and stopped their game. I was on the street side and a little to the rear of Samuel who had already raised his hand to greet the two neighborhood boys occupying the sidewalk. Maybe it was the presence of the strange boys in the street behind us that caused one of the neighborhood boys, the meaner and older of the two, to say what he did. Nobody in his right mind who knew Samuel would have said that within his reach. Not only was he strong and surprisingly quick, but behind those strangely shaped, dull eyes was a memory for hurts and nastiness. Bait Samuel from a safe distance and you could expect to escape immediate retribution, but you could be sure that he'd get you across the legs with that broom handle if he had to wait for weeks to do it. Bait Samuel up close and you were almost a sure thing for a bruise. Everybody knew it and nobody did it.

Nobody, that is, except a mean boy playing stepball who stopped his game long enough to acknowledge Samuel's raised hand and soft grunt with a loud question directed at me: "Hey, kid. This crazy your brother or your father?"

From that moment on, though years would elapse before I would read Shakespeare's line, I knew what it was for time to be out of joint. I was a spectator at a slow-motion film of arrested life. The boy's mouth was still open when Samuel's hand, the one that had been raised in greeting, moved slowly across the space intervening between itself and the boy's face, and closed its long, strong fingers around the skinny throat beneath the open mouth. The mouth stayed open and so did the eyes as the boy's hands rose to Samuel's wrist and then the whole boy—mouth, eyes, throat, hands—rose up in the air at the end of Samuel's outstretched arm. The eyes were already bugged and beginning to roll upward when I hit Samuel as hard as I could in the back of his strangely shaped head with the rock I had put in my pocket that morning in case I had to fight the boys on the next block.

When it was all over, when I got Samuel to the
barbershop and Ciro the barber had patched up his
bleeding head, I couldn't be sure of everything that
happened after I hit Samuel with the rock. All I could
be certain of was that he had dropped the kid and
started to turn toward me, then his knees had bent and
he had fallen sideways against me, knocking me off the
curb and into the gutter while he fell first to his knees
and then to his hands on the sidewalk. I don't know
what happened to the kid with the skinny throat and
the pop eyes, or to his three companies. I was all taken
up with watching Samuel on his hands and knees,
shaking his head back and forth while blood dripped
off the back of his neck to the pavement. I wanted to
run but I couldn't, not and leave him like that.

I knew he had a handkerchief because he was proud
of the initial "S" that was sewn on all of them and he
was always showing off the one he was carrying to
anyone who would look. And I knew he would be
taken care of if I could just get him to his feet,
press that handkerchief to his neck, and lead him
around the corner to Ciro's barbershop. This early in
the morning Ciro wouldn't have any other cus-
tomers—Samuel was always his first—and he knew
how to stop bleeding and take care of cuts. I knew all
this, but I was afraid. That boy had only called him a
name and Samuel had choked him; what would he do
to me for breaking his head with a rock? I sat in the
gutter and hoped that help would come. None did. It
was still too early for adults to be out on the street.

For thirty years now I have remembered the decision to stay and not to run as the first time in my life I went against my survival instincts. Getting up out of the gutter was nothing; going toward Samuel, putting my hands on his shoulders, helping him up and getting his handkerchief out of his pocket to press against his neck—those were the hardest things I ever did. All I could see was that boy's skinny throat, his open mouth and pop eyes, Samuel's long fingers squeezing together at the end of his outstretched arm. I was so frightened that I remember nothing of how we got to Ciro's from that bloody spot on the sidewalk. When Ciro took Samuel from me, I went into the back room of the barbershop, sat in an old barber's chair, and cried. And I wasn't ashamed for Ciro to come into the room and see me crying.

After we left, Ciro must have called Samuel's house from the pay telephone in his barbershop. I think Samuel never knew what happened—on the way home he kept touching his fingers to the bandage on the back of his head and grunting softly to himself —but the woman in his home knew all about it because she only asked me a couple of questions and then gave me those astounding five nickels when I had only been expecting one or maybe none at all. With the nickels in my hand and Samuel waving good-bye from the doorway, I could admit to myself as I ran down the steps to the street, rich, with all of Saturday before me, how near I had been to letting Samuel go up those steps by himself. I hadn't thought that anyone could understand the need to hit someone in the head with a rock.

John's Death

We walked slowly behind the bench that held the little man and his attendant. Soft, clean-shaven face, bullet head, unformed features, dull eyes—he was not Samuel, nor was the child who held tightly to me and walked close to my side. I felt the tension in the small hand as we passed the bench; suddenly, clearly, Samuel on one side of me and Kenny on the other, I knew why I was so beset with memories of that terrible Saturday morning in my childhood. Only a few years before I had watched the same child who now held a frisbee in one hand and my hand in the other, hold a large rock in both his hands and try to crush the skull of a neighboring boy rolling at play upon the grass. The attempt was inept. Perhaps it was meant to be, but it was one of the many signs that had led to his commitment. For the first time I recognized it as the real cause of my fears for my children if Kenny were to visit or to live in our home. But I could not let it be the only reality, nor could I make the decision alone. The child beside me was a dilemma for us all.

I drove back to the airport that evening with unsorted memories filling my head. Kenny with a rock raised in both hands high above his head, Samuel on his hands and knees, Kenny sitting on the sofa pressed against my side within the protective circle of my arm, Samuel's arm extended with the pop-eyed face at the end of his fingers, the unformed features and dull eyes of the little man sitting on the bench, Kenny in the foyer of his building saying good-bye to me, saying please come back please, watching me over his shoulder for as long as he could see me while the attendant

145

led him through the door first unlocked then locked again from the other side. . . . Outside, I looked up at lighted windows behind which lay sixteen beds arranged in two rows against the long walls of the dormitory room, each with its small chest of drawers, each occupied by one of fifteen other boys and Kenny, each uniform and neat and antiseptic and not like home. He had taken me to see them, both of us preceded by an attendant, had shown me his bed, had shown me his radio and his few toys kept safe from other hands (that sometimes could not control their anger) by being locked in a special room. We could not lock him in a special room. Our children could break like toys.

I came back in the early summer, this time not alone, driving east from Ann Arbor toward Cape Cod and the Atlantic Ocean. If we could no longer pretend that the lakes of northern Michigan were ocean enough for us, we could at least pretend to the children that we were not apprehensive about this visit to Kenny. We had arranged to keep him away from the institution overnight, to spend almost two days together in a nearby but not too near motel and restaurant complex where our connecting rooms, each with its own bath, would allow the three children to live in one room and give us use of the other.

For me the arrangement had been made possible by the conjunction of the man on the bench with Kenny walking beside me, the past finding place in present memory of Samuel and my tenth year. Paul's tenth year had begun in March. The coincidence was too great to ignore. Could I require him to be less than I had been when I wanted him to be more? Where is hope for the world in which a man creates his son in the diminished image of himself? Yet I would not have him poor to understand poverty, no more than I would have him mad to understand madness or dead to . . . he had outwatched the night of his brother's long dying and the watch had given his humanity depth and dimension before unpossessed. Beyond the obligation of protection, I had no right to stand between him and responsibility for his cousin.

I had momentarily forgotten that Kenny could be so shy, so vulnerable. The child I remembered had played frisbee, laughed, eaten a banana split, and proudly taken me to see his bed, chest, and toys. The one who stood before us, beaming attendant behind, was the fearful creature who had sat within the compass of my arm for an hour before he had strength to face the immoderate world. Martha hugged him to her, I embraced him, but still the great brown eyes absorbed the pinched face, all their attention upon the children who stood silently behind us.

"Arfie's waiting for us in the car," I said, knowing that Kenny remembered the dog from his visit to us in the year after his mother's death, before he was committed to the institution. Though the words were spoken in an imitation of hope, they were conceived in simple shame. That my children could not see the child's need, could not rise above their own reluctance, even if tinged with fear, could not reach out beyond themselves to another creature whose anguish must a thousand times devalue their fears. What had all the loving been for, years of impatient insistence that nothing mattered so much as care? How many times had I said that body, intellect, opportunity were accidents of birth and fortune, that human beings could know their worth only through the quality of attention and affection they were able to give? Remembered words choked me as my children stood there frozen and mute.

Three-year-old Lisa, suddenly and uncharacteristically, wanted to be carried. I stooped to pick her up and she dropped Paul's hand to reach up for me at the same time that Martha took Kenny's hand—leaving Paul standing by himself, staring soberly at Kenny whose eyes had never left him during our greeting. Lisa in my arms, I had already turned my back on the room to lead the way to our car when a small, familiar voice said clearly, "Arfie remembers you, Kenny. I told him we were coming to see you."

Holding a boy with each hand, conversation about Arfie's growth and color change since Kenny had seen him passing rapidly between the two of them, Martha walked past me into the hall. My shame at my son's selfish reluctance had disappeared in the face of a new lesson: he must be allowed to find his own fit. Because grip and embrace were often my means of attention and affection, they need not be his. Lisa and I brought up the rear as two boys built a bridge to each other that spanned more distance than arms could encompass.

I have seen so many beginnings unfollowed, so many conclusions unprepared, that I am always grateful for completion wherever I may find it. When I saw

Paul at thirteen and Kenny at nineteen sitting across from each other at their grandmother's kitchen table, Paul using flashcards to help Kenny learn to do arithmetic, Kenny having recently left the institution to live in his grandmother's care, I saw more than one step in the beginning of a struggle for rehabilitation that may extend through the rest of our lives. I saw as well the end of a beginning made initially in two rooms in a country motel, continued through a living room window, and extended down the slope of a university arboretum. A boy sitting patiently, gently with his cousin, flashing the same cards again and again, Paul is ready to do the caring work of a man.

"Caring work" is a phrase I first heard in my mother's mouth. It was her explanation to a neighbor of what I would be doing on a Saturday morning that would make me unavailable for an early trip to a nearby park. She was talking about my Saturday job with Samuel, which had her approval but for the payment that went with it. Looking to Samuel was caring work, she said, and no one was too young to learn about that. Nor should anyone expect payment for doing such work, but she supposed it was all right to accept what was offered as long as I didn't ask and was prepared to do without. At least, I thought to myself, I didn't ask.

Paul has been prepared and preparing for Kenny at his grandmother's kitchen table across three generations and through thirteen years. As I watched them together, the cards changing slowly, steady hands responding to nervous eyes and mouth unsure, gentle pace and words of reassurance, I could not help but think of the circularity of our existence, the visit to the neurosurgeon in Chicago almost a decade before, prognosis hopeless as winter with no growth to follow, changed now to a small Chicago suburban home alive with cautious tendrils of hope.

Paul began his caring work too early, responding to our grief with his reassuring presence when John took all we had to give. Held in my arms, he would pat my shoulder comfortingly; when we sat at the dinner table in silent exhaustion, removed from ourselves by despair, he would make wonderful, brave, childish efforts at beginning imaginative conversations like those we had once had the strength to initiate and enjoy.

"Go to sleep!" he had once said to me, commandingly, when he had found me in the middle of night dozing beside John's crib. "Go to your room and go to sleep. I'll be the watcher." I did as he said, sustained by the great presence that adversity had given him, sure of him, caught up in a reversal of roles so poignant that I could do no less than accept his offer. I knew then, instinctively, too tired to think, that it was better for him to assume some part of that impossible responsibility, even the unfitting part of midnight watcher, than to be a fearful spectator peering over a barrier of estrangement and guilt.

Though "guilt" may seem a strange and inappropriate word here, it appears to describe some significant part of a healthy child's response to disease and disability in other children. I cannot forget my own discomfortable feelings at my normality by contrast to some of the damaged creatures I knew as a child, and my own anguish for my friends whose parents did not like them or each other. My mother's response to my stories of unhappy children and families in our neighborhood was always some form of the question, "Why don't you do something about it?"

"Like what?"

"Does he have a mouth? Then let him come home and eat with you."

"He gets fed at home, Ma."

"Maybe that's all they give him. Bring him here. At least he won't be lonely when he eats."

We sometimes gave food, but we always gave attention. The realization that true privilege, the privilege that makes significant difference in the life of the holder, has much to do with attention and little to do with money, came as a jarring discovery to me when I found that the boy who lived in the biggest house in the neighborhood, the boy who had a pool table in his basement and boxing gloves in his room, whose closetful of clothes impoverished my two pairs of wash pants and two shirts, with a suit, shirt, and tie for Sunday school, was also the boy who would let my mother comb his hair and feed him unending meals. I do not like to remember that he had to find elaborate reasons for being at our house during the day, in spite of the fact that I wanted to play pool or box at his house, until my mother angrily pointed out that his need to be at our house was greater than mine to be at his—where no one was home during the day—and she didn't think much of someone who wouldn't take the time to un-

151

derstand that. Both my pool game and my self-regard suffered serious setbacks as I eased his way into my home.

I think my own anger was temporized by that memory a quarter of a century later when my son became deeply upset after I divided my attention between him and a classmate during an evening open-house at his elementary school. The other child's physical difference—his large head with protruding ears was unhappily emphasized by a very short haircut, his long slender legs hardly touched by ancient Bavarian walking shorts that may have fit him two years before—had been characterized by Paul after school one day with the phrase "real funny-looking."

"Do you tell him that?"

"No, I don't care if he's funny-looking."

"Does anybody?"

"Sure. He gets teased a lot."

"Why don't you stop it?"

"Me?" Face and voice incredulous, he turned toward me on the front seat of the car. The boy who was funny-looking waved tentatively at us as he passed on the sidewalk, green-gray faded walking shorts stretched tight on their shoulder straps with every step.

"You. He's in your class, isn't he?"

"Yes, but . . ."

I reminded him of the boy in our neighborhood upon whom a military-style brushcut had been inflicted by his father in preparation for a summer camping trip. With hairstyles growing longer, the boy

152

had looked like a visitor from a previous age and had known it, had been bitterly resentful and ashamed of his shorn appearance. His father had come to me to tell me of his gratitude to Paul who had understood his son's anguish, had insisted that the haircut looked fine and that he, Paul, was going to get one just like it when school was over for the year. Which was a blessed lie that put me in mind of Derek, his sister, and my uncle's battle flag. Some of which I recalled to Paul as we sat in our car in front of the school exit that disgorged children raised to believe that they were not their brothers' keepers.

"What can I do?"

"Don't let anybody be cruel to him. Not even once. Don't let it pass. Always say something about it."

"I'm not the teacher." Said looking away from me, through the window, at passing children free of unreasonable demands.

"That's why I'm talking to you. She's got twenty-five kids to look after. You've only got yourself. One more isn't so many."

"It's a lot if it's him."

Paul's teacher was an old acquaintance. I could have asked her if he was taking care of Otto, but I didn't. I wanted Paul to tell me himself, one way or another, and finally he did on the night of the open-house. Neither of Otto's parents were there, but he was— haircut, ill-fitting walking shorts, indirect glance, all the same but somehow worse because alone. Since Paul had both his parents in attendence upon him, I was able to pay court to Otto until he too was happily

153

leading an adult around the large room and out into the hall to the various places where his work was exhibited. The explosion came when I left Otto to accompany Paul to another room where refreshments were being served. With an habitual, unthinking gesture, I put my hand on his shoulder as we walked down the hall. Pushing my hand away, he hunched his shoulders and moved sideways beyond my reach. I was dumbfounded by the tears on his cheeks.

"What's the matter? What happened?"

"Nothing."

"Come on. Did I do something?"

"You're not his father!" A flash of real anger that illuminated the evening and made me understand.

"You've got both of us here and he's got nobody."

"I don't care. I'm going to let people be mean to him. He's a rat!"

"He's not. He's just awful lonely because everybody's got someone here except him."

"I'm the only one who's nice to him. He didn't have to take you. He could have taken somebody else."

"You've been looking after him?"

"Sure. Didn't you tell me to?"

"Caring work," an idea now embodied in the sociological concept of the extended family, is too seldom found anywhere else in a society of isolates who reproduce their isolation in children created in their own lonely image. Even the virtues of responsibility become transmuted into burdens and vices by the effects of isolation. "Be *responsible* for yourself," touchstone of independence and maturation, is distorted in memory and misshapen in practice until, no longer recognizable by the deeds it evokes, it becomes the last signpost of the singular society: "Be responsible for *yourself*."

From
Provincetown
to
Williamsburg...

San Francisco is not to be taken seriously. With a beautiful face and a frivolous heart, it is sometimes described by those who should know better as "the Paris of the West." Other than a department store which calls itself "City of Paris," no relationship is apparent. For people sensible enough to visit in midwinter, it is a visual delight and a fine base for exploring northern California.

Though not serious, San Francisco is wise. It has demonstrated its wisdom by banishing its poor to a large slum across the bay called Oakland, and by wearing the Pacific Ocean as its chief ornament. Unlike New York, which has turned its back on two great rivers, and Chicago, which lives in uneasy truce with Lake Michigan, San Francisco understands that the salt water which surrounds it on three sides is an incomparable setting for its beauty.

If San Francisco has banished its ugliness across the bay, Washington has hidden its sores in small streets behind great buildings whose whiteness is a symbol of the city's disease. Only one other capital city in the Western world has so consistently and so effectively disenfranchised its citizens through repression and spiritual robbery. No one who knows Washington, both free and slave, can read Joseph Conrad's description in *Heart of Darkness* of a European capital city as a "whited sepulchre" without making its modern American application. No one who knows Washington and values the country which it serves as capital could want it to represent America.

I have told my son that the Capitol, White House, monuments, and memorials are part of his inheritance and therefore to be known as one knows the coast at Monterey and Big Sur or Boston Common. I have told him that the great collections of the National Gallery, Smithsonian Institution, and Library of Congress belong to him, and he must assert his ownership by usage or his rights will perish by default. But I have also said to him that monuments, collections, meeting houses, and offices do not make a city. Such buildings may be permanent but their occupants are transient. In Washington, white transients in permanent buildings

160

ignore the squalor and decay of the ephemeral buildings that house the city's permanent residents, who are black. That, too, is part of Paul's inheritance. I want him to understand that those great buildings and monuments seem so soaring white because their base and frame are streetbound black. It is his responsibility, as it is mine, to alter that inheritance.

"If I were to see only one sight and visit only one place during my stay in America, what should they be?" Responding to those questions in a letter from an English friend, I suggested an overflight of Manhattan on a clear day and two weeks' residence in the heart of that island. Acknowledging my reply, she expanded her question: You've provided for a plane ride and a visit, she said. Now you must tell me where in America to use a train, an auto, and a boat. Though I kept up my part by advising a train ride through the Rockies from Denver to San Francisco, an elliptical motor tour of the Shenandoah Valley between Harpers Ferry on the north and Lexington on the south, and a leisurely sail down the California coast from San Francisco Bay to San Simeon Point, my heart was not in the game. Had I been English, French, Danish, Italian, or a hundred other nationalities besides, I would have sent her, with pride leading the way, to my capital city. But because I am an American, ashamed of the oblivious white face of the center of my government, I sent her elsewhere.

In this case, elsewhere was the capital city of mid-twentieth-century Western civilization. By overflight, shank's mare, or subway, it is a city of immense excitements, dangers, disappointments, joys—the scale almost superhuman, the people so endlessly varied as to have gathered from distant parts of the earth. A very small cross section of this variety, a spring growth, Martha and I among them, stood before the entrance to the Museum of Modern Art a few minutes before its opening, rapt attention from nearly all of us given to a young man who played Tchaikovsky's Violin Concerto as though he too had lived in Russia during the second half of the nineteenth century.

It was Tchaikovsky's Concerto that caused a delicate contemporary critic to complain about violins being beaten black and blue to satisfy uncontrolled composition and unrestrained passion. The young man who played it for us on a bright, hazy spring morning on Fifty-third Street was as controlled as he was unrestrained. When the piece was ended, we joined the warm round of applause, put some coins into his violin case, and filed through the opened doors into the museum.

Perhaps it was because we had been away from our children for almost a week, or it may have been his pleasant, open face and the violin that seemed an extension of his arm. Whatever the reason, an hour later when I passed through the lobby on my way to the outdoor sculpture garden and heard the sound of his violin through the front doors that were closing behind a group of schoolchildren, I followed a strong impulse and left the building to find him playing for a depleted audience of museum-goers and casual passersby. He was not as good with Telemann as he had been with Tchaikovsky, but he was a fiddler who deserved better than his vanishing audience. By the time the piece was done, two young girls, an old derelict, and I were the only ones available to supply applause and I was the only one to supply money. I handed him the bill instead of dropping it into his violin case.

"Hey, thanks. Thanks a lot! I can really use that."

"You earned it with the Tchaikovsky Concerto."

"I played that an hour ago. Were you here then?"

"Yes. I've been in the museum for a while. I wanted to give you that before, but I didn't want to embarrass anybody."

"Five dollars is a lot. A lady gave me ten dollars once, but she was high on something." A pause, then carefully: "Say, you're not a homosexual, are you?"

"No, I'm not."

"That's good. I need that five dollars, but I go for girls. Why'd you give it to me, anyway?"

"Because of a lot of things, I guess. When you're playing, you look like my son and sound like my father. That's worth five bucks any time."

"Come on. You haven't got a kid my age."

"No. I could, but I don't. He's probably ten years younger than you are but he's been playing for so long that the violin looks like an extension of his arm when he handles it, the same as it does with you."

"Is he good?"

"No. He's terrible, but he likes it. I guess that's what really matters."

"Say, you're pretty cool. People tell me all the time about how great their kids are. You're the first one

163

who ever said his kid was terrible, and you didn't get sore when I asked if you were queer."

Because I'd made a friend, to whom I spoke for another few minutes before returning to the museum, I didn't respond to his praise with the blame that leaped immediately to my tongue. I didn't get sore when he'd asked me if I were homosexual, but I might have if he'd asked me if I were queer. It's a word I've hated since high school when I met the first homosexual I'd ever known, a boy who needed protection from himself as much as he needed protection from the bullies who made his life a hallway hell after he lost and they found his diary confessing his love for one of the boys on the football team. I told my son about him when he picked up a friend's language to describe a cruising homosexual in Provincetown.

"Look at that queer!" Paul was sitting behind us in the middle of the back seat, his sister playing in the rear of the stationwagon as we drove slowly down Provincetown's main street.

"No," I said, adjusting the rear-view mirror so that he could see himself in it. "Look at this one."

He was startled and thoughtful. "What did I say?" he asked, as our eyes met in the mirror.

"He's homosexual, if that's what you mean by queer, and that gives him enough problems in this world without you calling him names."

"It's just a word."

"Maybe to you but not to him and not to me. Anyway, it's an ugly word and you can do better."

— From Provincetown to Williamsburg —

Provincetown is not only at the far end of Route 6 on Cape Cod, it is also at the far end of sexual life in the United States. A small but highly visible percentage of year-round and summer population is both gay and liberated, at least from the need to hide their homosexuality, if not from the need to flaunt it. The particular specimen of gay humanity that had provoked Paul's comment was a slender young man dressed in a tiny pair of shorts, a golden amulet, sandals, and shoulder wallet. However remarkable his clothes may have been, they were almost commonplace by comparison to his movements as he walked. Infinitely graceful, sinuous, and feminine in the extreme, he was a phenomenon that had to be dealt with in the life of a boy approaching puberty. A half-block farther along the street, a group of homosexual men gave me the opportunity I wanted.

"Look at the one in the lace pants."

"I see him."

"He's queer. The same way you or I would be queer if we wore lace pants. Queer like in odd or peculiar. Not like in homosexual. Do you see the difference?"

"I guess so. Do you know any homosexuals?"

"Sure. So do you, but you don't know it yet."

"You mean some of my friends are qu . . . homosexuals?"

"No. I don't mean that. The ones you know are friends or acquaintances of mine, but they don't advertise themselves like the one back there who walked like a sexy woman or this one with the lace pants."

"So how do you know about them?"

"I don't really know, not for sure. They don't ask me about my sex habits and I don't ask them about theirs. But I think I know, from their conversation and their company and sometimes from the way they handle their bodies or their faces or their hands. It's a lot of little things, I guess, and none of it matters until you see it all together like here on Commercial Street."

"Why does it matter here?" Trust him to ask the hard question. We dropped off Martha and Lisa to shop, then left Commercial Street and drove out the fishing pier to its end where we could see the new breakwater, the boats at anchor in its lee, and behind us, stretching away on both sides, the extraordinary beauty of the village itself. *Why does it matter here?* The question was as uncomfortable as the fact of homosexuality, and yet I had to try to answer it for both of us. A small troop of gulls rose effortlessly on the soft evening air. I watched them sink to the water's surface and rise to sink again. No signs of guidance were forthcoming.

"That's a hard question. I'll have to tell you about Beverly in order to answer it."

"Who's she?"

"He."

"That's a girl's name."

"In America, mostly it is. But not always. In England it's often a man's name. The Beverly I knew was a boy who was in my high school class for three years."

"Was he a fairy?"

"Are you a kike?"

166

— From Provincetown to Williamsburg —

"What's that?"

"A nasty name for a Jew."

"Fairy's like queer?"

"Would you like to be called a fairy or a queer because you were sexually different from most people?"

"Was he a homosexual?"

"Yes."

"How'd you know? Did he love you?"

"No, but he told me himself. And he wrote in his diary that he was in love with a boy on our football team." No context more appropriate than Provincetown for telling Paul about Beverly, whose mother had given him an equivocal name and then raised him by herself to fulfill his ambiguous promise. When the homeroom teacher in our all-male high school had called our names from the class roll for the first time, we had all turned in our seats to look at the boy named Beverly. None of us had ever seen one before.

Even if he wasn't comfortable when we stared at him, at least he must have expected it. Any boy with long bleached-blond hair, wearing glasses with green frames, would certainly have expected to be stared at in 1945. I was so astounded at the sight that my jaw dropped and I couldn't shift my eyes. I had sometimes said that a boy who wouldn't fight or who was afraid to play football on a rocky playground was a fairy, but it was just a word. I had never known a boy who was different in kind, as was this one who sat so blondly in the back of the room.

Our homeroom teacher couldn't remember our

names unless we sat according to an alphabetical seating chart. When we had been shuffled about, I found myself seated across the aisle from Beverly with the long blond hair and green-framed glasses. Worse, I found that four out of five of my teachers could not operate without an alphabetical seating chart, which meant that Beverly and I were day-long neighbors whenever both of us were in school.

"Did it feel funny sitting next to him?" We had walked along the pier a hundred yards back toward town in order to see more closely the handling and docking of a big commercial sailing vessel. The water darkened as we watched, seeming to lose the light of the setting sun to the great white sails that threw their shadows over the mooring. Then the boat made its last tack, light came once again across the still water, and we sat on a concrete bench to watch the well-practiced drill of her crew.

"It did at first. After a while, though, it felt just like sitting next to you now."

"Come on, Daddy. I'm not queer." With an effort I passed over the ugly word that came so easily to his lips.

"Why should it feel any different? Long hair and green glasses don't matter for very long."

"Did he wear lace pants or walk funny like that other one did?"

"He didn't wear lace pants and he didn't walk funny except sometimes when he was with his friends." Our large high school had four or five boys in other grades and classes whose relationship to Beverly was marked by their long, bleached-blond hair and green-framed glasses. They formed a group before and after school, during lunch period, sometimes between classes, and always during speeches, pep rallies, and concerts in the auditorium. It was during one of our auditorium assemblies that disaster struck Beverly and caused us to become friends.

When the lights went down in the auditorium and up on the stage, when behind the curtain the theme song of our school jazz band rose toward a crescendo, I stood and began applauding with the rest. The band was good and the occasion was a pep rally on the day before the annual Thanksgiving renewal of one of the oldest high school football rivalries in the nation. When the curtains opened upon jazz band, football team, principal, and various functionaries, I forgot about everything else except football and school spirit. So, unfortunately, did Beverly, sitting with his friends elsewhere in the auditorium, who afterwards tried to reconstruct what had happened and thought that the diary must have fallen from his lap when he rose to applaud the band and the team.

Before the lights went down, he and his friends had been passing their diaries around among themselves. The next time Beverly remembered that he had a diary was when he went to his locker at the beginning of lunch period to get his coat. Three boys were waiting for him, one holding his diary and reading aloud from it to the other two. Because lockers were also alphabetically assigned, and our lunch period was the same, I was just around the corner at my own locker when I heard screaming followed by laughter, a thud, and sobbing. I went to see what had happened.

"Hey, Fader. Listen to this." Beverly was up against a locker, held there with one hand by Aaron, a boy my size who held a book in his other hand and wanted me to listen to something. I knew him, but I didn't know the other two except as familiar faces.

"What's that?"

"It's Beverly's diary. Listen to this." I don't know what I would have done if I had found that diary. Maybe I too would have read it and told the world about it. But whatever I would have done, I wouldn't have done what he was doing then. The shock and terror on Beverly's face made me feel sick. What Aaron was reading made me feel even sicker. Imitating Beverly's light, nasal voice, he was reading a passionate confession of love for the senior star of our football team. I listened to the brief passage in shocked silence. When he was done, I was the first one to speak.

"Okay. So let him go." I was surprised at the harshness of my own voice.

"He tried to scratch me. The creep." The creep who had called Beverly a creep, which I had no doubt he was, especially after hearing the diary, shook Beverly once against the lockers, banging his head, then released him. Like a demented terrier, without hesitation and without warning, Beverly grabbed for his diary, missed, and scratched the boy's hand with his long nails.

"Son of a bitch! I'll kick your ass!" Throwing the

diary at his friends, he reached for Beverly, who promptly kicked him in the knee, ducked under his arm, and dove for the diary that was still on the floor. Before he could reach it, one of the two boys kicked it toward me. I picked it up, reflexively, not wanting it and not knowing what to do with it or the bad situation developing in front in me. Beverly was scrambling to his feet when Aaron, with all the fury of a scratched hand and bruised knee, hit him on the side of the head. Had it been a solid punch, Beverly wouldn't have cared for a while what happened to his diary. But it was a roundhouse right above the ear that caught Beverly moving away and knocked him to the floor between us without doing much damage. He lay there for a moment, all of us enmeshed in one of those stupefying silences that always punctuate a real fight, then burst into tears. It was a terrible sight and sound.

"Get up, you fairy bastard. I'll teach you to kick and scratch."

"You've already taught him. Leave him alone." Had I said that? I was surprised to hear my own voice, but the creature lying on the floor between the lockers, knees drawn up, one arm outstretched while the other protected the side of his head where he had been struck, had been taught enough and more than enough. All I wanted was to talk the crisis away. I had no desire to fight Aaron to protect Beverly. What would I be fighting for? A fairy who kicked and scratched, a diary that was sick? But I knew what was going to happen as though I'd seen it in a movie.

— From Provincetown to Williamsburg —

"Give me the diary," The back of the hand that he reached toward me for the little book had three stripes of blood on it.

"Come on. What do you want it for?" He didn't know yet what I had just discovered: I wasn't going to give it to him.

"Because I want it. Give it here." What else could he do? As long as Beverly stayed on the floor, he was safe. And he looked like he might stay there forever. If Aaron's friends hadn't seen everything, I probably could have talked him out of it. But with Beverly on the floor and me with the diary, his friends watching and Aaron having already had the worst of it, we were all caught in a confrontation that could have only one kind of conclusion. I put the little book in the back pocket of my jeans.

"Forget it. He's had enough."

"You want some?" We had arrived where we had been heading ever since I had told Aaron to let him go. We both knew what the answer was.

"All you've got. After school, next to the parking lot."

"Right now. I want that diary right now."

"Drop dead, jerk. You're not dumb enough to think you can take it from me by yourself. Get your brother and I'll get my cousin and we'll see who gets the diary after school." Fighting in the locker area was sure to get us caught by one of the faculty members who patrolled the halls during lunch periods. Getting caught meant getting after-school detention for at least a week, maybe two. Since my cousin was banking

172

From Provincetown to Williamsburg

and I was dealing the big after-school blackjack game, detention would cost me serious money. Aaron was a notorious bully who was said never to pick a fight unless his older brother, a senior, was there to back him up. My cousin was even bigger than I was. It would be a real battle.

I never found out how the battle would have turned out. I looked down at Beverly to tell him to stop sobbing and get up off the floor. As I looked down, Aaron charged at me across Beverly's body. I had been careless because I was so sure that I could take him and that he knew it. My hands were still at my sides as he started to swing. He would have had me cold if Beverly hadn't lashed out with his feet and caught him on both shins just as he lunged for me. Aaron hit the lockers to my right, I hit him once with a weak left hook as he fell, Beverly was on his feet and running for his life down the hall, and Aaron's two friends vanished around the lockers on my left. I heard them pounding down the cross corridor away from the one Beverly had taken.

"You still want me and Jerry after school?"

"Forget it." He was sitting against the lockers, blood on his tee shirt where he had fallen against his hand.

"Leave the fairy alone or it's you and me." When he said nothing, I got my lunch out of my locker and left. I wasn't anxious to wait around long enough to see if he could work up his nerve again.

Beverly was where I knew I'd find him, in the drugstore on the corner of Alameda and Thirty-third having lunch with his friends. While I ate my lunch with my cousin in the school cafeteria, I had decided what to do. The part of the diary that Aaron read had convinced me I didn't want to read any more, but giving it back wasn't as simple as it sounds. After lunch, Jerry and I went down the hill to the corner drugstore. Through the window I could see Beverly and his friends sitting together in the back of the store. They were talking so intently that they didn't see us come in.

"Hey, Beverly." I had spoken more loudly than I intended to. All conversation stopped as five blond heads turned to look at me. "Come on outside for a minute. I want to talk to you."

"No. We can talk right here."

"That's all right with me. You want everybody to hear, I don't care."

"Everybody's going to hear anyway, aren't they?"

"You mean from that jerk Aaron?"

"I mean from you. You're the one who's got my diary. He's just a dumb bully. But you've got my diary. Or did you give it back to him after I ran away?"

"Come on, Daniel. You can't help a queer like him." If my cousin had a short fuse, so did Beverly.

"Queer! Fairy! That's all you can say. You're both as dumb as he is."

"Look, Beverly, I'm sorry about what happened at the lockers. I didn't want to hear that creep read from your diary. I don't give a shit who you love and who you don't. But you're the one who's dumb if you don't know who your friends are. Maybe I should just give him your diary and forget about it."

"Don't do that. Please. I'm sorry. Please give it back to me."

— From Provincetown to Williamsburg —

"I can't do that either. That's what Jerry and I've been talking about. Aaron's pretty brave with his brother around. If they think we've got your diary, they may get brave enough to try us out. But you're safe as long as we've got it and you don't. They may run their mouths on you, but I don't think they'll do anything else. So Jerry and I will keep your diary in a safe place. I promise we won't read it and we'll give it back at the end of the year."

"What do I have to do so you won't read it and you'll give it back?"

"What do you mean . . . ?" Suddenly I knew what he meant. "You creep. You're disgusting. You and your whole bunch of fairies. Here's your sick diary. I hope Aaron slaps you around every time he sees you." I took the diary out of my pants pocket and dropped it on the table. As Jerry and I walked out of the drugstore, he was telling me that that's what you got for being nice to a queer.

Paul couldn't contain himself any longer: "I thought you just said 'queer' and 'fairy' were ugly words and I shouldn't say them. You and Jerry used to say them."

I admitted that we did, and then I told him the end of the story. How Beverly had come to me and apologized, how he had explained that nobody, not even his mother or his aunts, were ever nice to him just to be nice to him. They were like all the rest, he said, always wanting something from him. He talked a lot, and most of it was angry and pitiful, but the saddest part was when he asked me if I didn't mind being seen with him on the school grounds in plain sight of every-

175

body. His question made me think back five years to Samuel and how ashamed I'd been to be known as his companion on Saturday mornings when I first took him to the barbershop. I told Beverly about Samuel, with what I recognized years later as the kind of well-meant cruelty possible to a fifteen-year-old, talking about the two of them as people somehow like each other who didn't have to be like me to be my friends. Because Beverly saw himself in the same way as aberrant and outcast, as a Samuel without brain damage or broom handle, he accepted my awkward analogy. Our friendship began with that conversation and lasted throughout our high school years.

"So why do you get mad when I say queer?"

"Because it can hurt somebody so much."

"But I wouldn't say it to a . . . I mean, to a person who liked men instead of ladies."

"How could you always be sure? A few homosexuals may look like Beverly and his friends, but most look like you and me. You can only be sure by keeping words like 'queer' and 'fairy' out of your mouth all the time. You know what Beverly told me about them? He said every time he heard them he wanted to cry. Because he couldn't, he'd get angry instead and do crazy things."

The sun had set across the bay as we talked; we could see Martha walking toward us with Lisa. They were the only people at the foot of the pier, their size diminished by their isolation against the buildings behind them. As I watched them grow on their approach, a group of men appeared in the farther dis-

176

tance beyond them, also walking toward us, the gait
and exaggerated gestures of a few identifying their
sexual bent. Their appearance caused me to remember Paul's question that had evoked the past and
memories of Beverly.

"You remember asking me why I said being a
homosexual matters here when it doesn't matter in
other places?"

"You never told me why."

"Look at the group of men walking behind Mother
and Lisa. What do you see?"

"They're homosexuals."

"How do you know?"

"By the way some of them walk."

"Yes, and if you were close enough, you could probably tell by the way they talk, too. It was the same with
Beverly and his friends. Except for their bleached hair
and the green glasses some of them wore, they looked
pretty much like everybody else when they were alone
or with people who weren't homosexual. But they
always got like that when they were together. When I
asked Beverly about it, he claimed he was always the
same. After a while, though, he admitted that he
wasn't. He didn't know why, he just wasn't."

The group of men had passed Martha and Lisa, who
had stopped to look down at the ebbing tide from the
edge of the pier, and were now near enough to us to be
overheard. Absorbed in themselves, they were apparently unaware of our presence on the bench. As they
passed, I turned to Paul: "See the man in the white
pants with the scarlet overshirt and headband?"

"Sure. You can't miss him."

"You could if you flew here from Boston with him.
I've seen him several times when I've flown back on a
Friday; once we sat together and talked. That looks
like a different man walking there, but he's the same.
When he's with other homosexuals, he behaves differently. That's why it matters here when it wouldn't
matter somewhere else."

"I don't like them. I won't call them queers or fairies,
but I'm not going to like them."

"They won't care, and neither will I. Maybe someday
you'll know a boy or a man like Beverly, and you'll feel
differently."

"Maybe I'll feel sorry for him and be nice to him, but
I won't like him."

Because I couldn't think of anything else to say, I
was grateful for the arrival of Martha, trailing Lisa
behind, who asked us what we had been doing while
we waited for them.

"Watching the big sailboat dock," Paul said, too
quickly, looking at me for corroboration.

"Yes," I said, "and talking about different people."
Paul's small smile was as tentative as my own.

To give the gift of a place is no easier than to give the
gift of an attitude. Both gifts can be impositions,
gracelessly given and reluctantly received. Just as
forms of divinity and sexuality are essentially private
possessions, so are the places of the individual past
private to their possessors, rarely meaningful or even
communicable to the unpossessed. My brother and I

can share with each other the streets and alleys, the schoolyards and ballfields of our youth. We have walked through old neighborhoods and schoolyards still safe for men on foot, and we have driven slowly, windows up and doors locked, through other playgrounds and battlegrounds of our past that do not welcome our return. For me the most personal loss is our neighborhood poolroom, where we no longer go because it is a black and dangerous place for a white man to be, no matter how good a stick he shoots.

A fat and dully gleaming bowl, reflecting in its plump sides the room beneath it, standing on a large, oiled-wood cube with an unengraved metal plaque upon it (cube, plaque, and bowl surmounted by the figure of a man with a pool cue in his hands, leaning forward as though about to execute a shot on a table mercifully omitted from the tableau), all rising from the marble ledge of one of the high casement windows in my basement study. On the ledge next to this monument and summary of my youth are two cups, mementos of championships in table games arbitrarily designated as intercollegiate sports, games called straight-rail and three-rail billiards which are played in college by former poolroom hustlers who have stopped playing pool because of the lack of competition and have gone straight-rail. The burnished bowl may appear to be the nadir of the trophy-maker's art, which it is, but it is also the zenith of my athletic career. Lemuel Gulliver was no more astounded at his discovery of Lilliput than I was to find that national intercollegiate athletic championships are awarded

179

to straight shooters who have confined much of their adolescent lives within the boundaries of a sixty by one-hundred-and-eight-inch table surfaced with slate, surrounded by rubber sides, and covered with green baize.

Gulliver and I were not the only ones astounded at our discoveries. My father was dumbstruck by my phone call from the student union at Ohio State (where regional winners from all over the United States had gathered to hustle for the national championship) announcing to him, my family, and all others in the eagerly awaiting world, the identity of the 1952 intercollegiate billiards champion. "You're *what?*" and "Good God!" were the extent of his immediate responses before he handed the telephone to my mother, to whom my championship meant only a little more than nothing at all. As he told me later, a national intercollegiate billiards championship was not one of the accomplishments he'd anticipated when he saw his son off to college. It was something, he said, that required a little more time for adjustment than a phone call allowed.

Poolrooms and bowling alleys, with their inevitable gambling, had been very sore subjects in my home. When I had learned that a good bowler and better pool player could earn a steady weekly income, I gave up most of my participation in sports my father regarded as wholesome and manly, and pursued the money I coveted more than manhood. Intuitive of my feelings, gentle, displaced by the explosive geometry of a world war that produced a new era and new children, my father did what he could to dissuade me from a pursuit that was distasteful and mysterious to him. In return for his gentleness, I shielded him and my mother from knowledge of my underground life.

Notes from Underground may have been a metaphorical title for Dostoevsky, but *underground* was reality for me. Knocko and Hotchie's poolroom, next to the gas station on the corner of Ayrdale and Liberty Heights, was the basement of a building that had a laundry and dry cleaning establishment as well as a restaurant upstairs. No one downstairs really cared what was upstairs, for the steep wooden steps that led from the separate ground-level entrance to the swinging doors of the poolroom, were steps into a better world than those remaining upstairs and outside could know. The rush of security that met me as I descended the narrow, noisy staircase was equaled only by the comfort of entering the front door of my home at five thirty on a winter evening.

Five thirty was our non-negotiable dinner hour because my father worked in the evenings, as well as in the mornings and afternoons, and had to be back on the street by six thirty. To be at home by five thirty meant leaving the poolroom at five ten to walk home, five fifteen to walk and run alternate blocks, or five twenty to race across all nine blocks through the gathering night. Since it was most often five twenty before I ran through the swinging doors to bound frantically up the stairs, envying all those who did not have to be home at five thirty or did not have to be home at all, I learned to perform several unusual acts

181

of survival on the dead run. Most important was washing my hands.

As any habitual pool player will tell you, the middle finger on the left hand (for right-handed people) will identify the hustler or recently hustled, if water has not obliterated the sign. For many years the sign was always blue, though recently the possibilities have been increased by both green and brown. Blue, brown, or green, the identifying sweep of color between the knuckle and first joint of the middle finger comes from colored chalk applied to the tip of the pool cue to promote friction in its contact with the cue ball. When the cue stick, in rhythmic preparation for striking the cue ball, is moved back and forth through the enclosed "bridge," which in fact is more like a tunnel created of the circled thumb and forefinger bisected by the extended middle finger, some chalk from its tip is bound to rub off on the segment of the middle finger over which it passes. My dexterity at washing my hands while running dates from the dinner at which my father revealed how he could usually tell when I had been in the poolroom. As he spoke, he leaned across the table and picked up my hand with the blued finger for all to see. Though I had washed my hands before dinner, I had soaped only palms and fronts of fingers; as my brother once said to our mother, "People who eat with the backs of their hands should have to wash the backs of their hands." To that select group he could have added those who shoot pool.

To my banker, who took care of my money, soliciting and covering all the action we could afford before a game, then collecting or paying off afterward, receiving in return a portion of my winnings or absorbing an equal portion of my losses, fell the responsibility of having three wet paper towels and two dry ones ready for my five-twenty exodus. Dry towels in my pockets, wet towels in my hands, I could race down Ayrdale toward Sequoia while using a wet one on the back of my left hand, a wet one on my face which often had a blue chalk stain from inadvertent contact with the cue stick, and a wet one on the front of my pants which usually bore powder marks from the talcum we all used to assure the cue a smooth passage through our fingers. A dry one for my face, a dry one for my hand, both wet and dry disposed of in transit, and I was fit for household inspection. Once I was satisfied that the scheme worked, I always made a point of washing my hands with my father at the kitchen sink. The moment was companionable and reassuring for both of us.

Each of the eight tables in the poolroom had its own special characteristics, and I was familiar with the quirks and foibles of each. Just as a good outfielder learns every dip and rise in the outfield of every baseball park he plays in, so that he can chart his position in relation to the fences while running at full speed and paying conscious attention only to the moving ball, in the same way a house hustler must learn the idiosyncrasies of every table in his home poolroom. While one table—the front one in Knocko's (Hotchie died young)—is often reserved for the heavy games because it has the best cloth, the truest rails, and the smoothest bed, all home tables are potential money farms and the wise house hustler cultivates their every furrow. Since pits and grooves in the beds of all but the number one table are as inevitable as worn cloth and dead rails, the man who knows the furrows has an edge. I have seen important early money change hands in a contest where the significant difference between two players was that only one knew the table rolled slightly toward one corner pocket and away from another.

When I returned to Knocko's for a party to celebrate my championship with sandwiches from upstairs on me (twenty dollars worth, supplied courtesy of Brunswick Company who put up the trophy together with money to engrave it—which is why it is still unengraved today) and soft drinks on Knocko, no one was surprised that I had hitchhiked to Ohio State from Cornell a month before the tournament, spending a three-day weekend on a sofa in a friend's fraternity house while I played hours of billiards on all the tables in the new Student Union. Every serious hustler from my poolroom would have thought of doing the same, even if he had been unable to arrange it. Why play if you didn't want to win? The question was our credo, and we had each spent our adolescence searching for an edge. In their view, as in mine, the eight-hundred-odd miles of my preliminary round trip between Ithaca and Columbus was not too far to search.

The party at Knocko's was held after-hours on a Saturday night, sandwiches and drinks on top of the cash register counter, pinball machine, and bleacher seats, two dozen familiar hustlers and hangers-on, all

184

dominated by that remarkable trophy from its central position on number one, the heavy action table, which had first been brushed and spread with its protective cover. Knocko made an eloquent speech, brief, direct, punctuated by several elegant obscenities which were duly admired and applauded, then gave me the floor for my acknowledgment. Because he had ended with the wonderful irony of local-boy-makes-good, his final gesture pointing toward the trophy (gleaming beneath the hot overhead light) as he said, "Now ain't that a mother!" I was inspired to begin and end with the observation that since I owed everything to Knocko's Emporium and therefore my trophy belonged to everybody in the room as well as to many who had left behind their money if not their bodies (selective laughter; I owned a piece of a number of my guests), I thought it only right to announce that I was leaving it on permanent display in the room and nobody should steal it because it wasn't worth anything in any hock shop anywhere. They should take my word for it, I said, because I had tried to hock it in Columbus, Ithaca, and Baltimore with no success. When Knocko led the applause, I picked up the trophy and put it in his arms. My clearest memory of that night is the vision of Knocko, corned-beef sandwich in one big hand and Pepsi-Cola in the other, his arms wrapped around the trophy, grasping it to his chest. I hope the sight would have pleased the Brunswick people as much as it pleased me.

That same trophy, removed from permanent display two and a half years later when I went to Europe

185

in the army, stored for a decade in the basement of my parents' home, then in the basement of our first home in Ann Arbor, unpacked at Paul's request when he had discovered it while playing among cartons and boxes, now stands in the high casement window of my study, reflecting a distorted image of the desk, chair, and shelves of books that have replaced pool and billiards in my life. The room that it reflects is long and wide. Its exact length escapes me because it was clearly long enough, but I know its width to the inch—fourteen feet five inches from wall to wall—because I could not be satisfied with less than fourteen feet four inches, obtained by tearing out the closets which lined one side of the room when we bought the house last year. The extra inch gives me just a little more than the minimal necessary space for the stroke of my cue at either side of the full-sized billiard table that occupies the center of my study.

For five minutes, ten at most, I pick up my cue and play the wonderfully complex, angular, self-contained game of three-rail billiards. Perhaps I play for twenty minutes a day, sometimes with Paul but most often by myself, recreating in my imagination the poolrooms, opponents, games, even the shots with which I won or lost. For moments brief and fleeting I can recreate the haven of green cloth and ivory balls that once allowed me to retreat from a world where sanctuary was hard to find. My father understood that, years ago, and now I must make the same effort, pain of possession ungiven and inheritance lost, to understand and accept my son's indifference. Because I could not give him

— From Provincetown to Williamsburg —

Knocko's poolroom, life caught and time stopped in a basement with eight pool tables, it matters less that I cannot give him a single billiard table in a basement study.

Let the gifts flow the other way. We learned to sail together five years ago; now he is becoming a better sailor than I, and takes responsibility for improving me. He is impatient with my desire merely to sail across the wind, thrumm of taut sails and soft hiss of the planing hull in my ears, face to the sun, salt water drops suspended in air, coming from nowhere that I may go toward nothing. He surges to compete, tightening down to race, vital, excited, intolerant.

"Come on! Trim your sail."

"Who are we racing?"

"Don't you want to do it the right way?"

No, I think but do not say. His eyes move knowingly between set of sails and pattern of wind on water, one hand lightly on the tiller while the other grasps the mainsheet. He is my son and my companion and I cannot tell him that I do not care, that I race with no man and none with me. I have competed, my God how I have competed!, and now I want no more.

"Shit!" he says to himself, believing I cannot hear, as the boat he is racing, though its crew is innocent of the knowledge, tacks toward the mouth of Blackfish Creek where he does not want to go. He looks for other quarry as I angrily trim the jib before he tells me to, not liking the reflection of my poolroom language in his mouth nor the orders harshly laid upon my ears. I will throw a dozen fastballs past him on the softball field, muscle him under the boards on the basketball court, wipe him out on the pool table. I will . . . I will lie back in the sun and salt spray, close my eyes and feel the sea about me. I will be forty-four before he is fourteen.

Because we are accumulative, both richer as individuals and unique as a species in remembering ourselves, I want to give my son as legacy of the past some part of those people, places, and objects which have brought a special richness to my life. It troubles me greatly that so few have survived: Vietnam has depressed the coin of Fort McHenry and our flag, though I believe the devaluation temporary and the coin usable for purchase in the future. Less redeemable is the heritage of slavery hidden just behind the urban rot that has robbed me and therefore my son of Knocko's poolroom as well as most of the alleys and schoolyards of my youth. Derek is dead of a stroke in his bed, Knocko murdered by a robber in his poolroom, the heart of Baltimore so reconstructed that the rhythm of its once familiar beat is now alien to me. . . .

I hear the question. No, I do not want Paul to relive any part of the life that has belonged to me, but I believe he cannot fully belong to himself until he has seen himself reflected in the mirror of my past, which is also his. Seen from the broadest angle, the burnished bowl on the marble windowsill in my study reflects more than a billiard table, more than desk, books, and chair. It reflects one core sampling of America in the

—From Provincetown to Williamsburg —

mid-twentieth century, between Great Depression and Glorious Fourth, ten years of poverty and two hundred of nationhood, for better in peace and for worse in three wars, a nation belonging to both of us which we may give as a gift to each other because it is a nation different for each of us.

Derek's greatest unfulfilled wish was to travel by boat, by sailing boat with an auxiliary motor, southeast down the Patapsco River to the great column of the Chesapeake Bay, then south down the bay by easy stages, camping and exploring along the way, until the Chesapeake combined its waters at Norfolk with the Atlantic Ocean. Unlike the bay which turned east, we would turn west through Hampton Roads, between Norfolk on the south and Hampton/Newport News on the north, then northwest up the James River to Jamestown Island. There we would beach and secure our boat in order to explore an area which meant a great deal to Derek—the site of the first permanent English settlement in the United States. After completing our exploration, he said, we would walk a northerly route overland to Williamsburg, the colonial capital in process of restoration by John D. Rockefeller, Jr. According to Derek, the only true words Franklin Roosevelt ever spoke were those in which he described colonial Williamsburg's central thoroughfare, Duke of Gloucester Street, as the most historic avenue in America. Since FDR was next to the Lord in my family's pantheon and next to the devil in Derek's, I did not tell him that I was glad to take the President's word for the importance of Gloucester Street.

— From Provincetown to Williamsburg —

How many hours did we sit on the benches of Mt. Vernon Place, in bright sunlight reflected from the first Washington Monument, watching the slow movement of shadow across grass and cobblestone toward Peabody Conservatory, reading the map of our journey to Williamsburg? Derek was elated at the prospect of returning to the water which had held so much of his life. He would speak the names of landfalls and outflowing rivers like a litany which itself would evoke the journey, would bring the end of war and peace enough to allow us to float down the Chesapeake to America's heartland. The phrase was his—"America's heartland"—taken perhaps from the colonial history that was his favorite reading, a phrase as ordinary in his mouth as it is now rare upon the printed page.

Keeping land close on our starboard side, we planned to sail down the western shore of the Chesapeake after emerging from the Patapsco between the sentinel ghosts of Fort Howard on the north and Fort Smallwood on the south. At Bodkin Point we would sail south down the bay, soon passing Gibson Island and the entrance to the Magothy River before rounding Sandy Point, crossing the mouth of the outflowing Severn, and making our first landfall at Annapolis. There we would visit America's most important institution but for the Capitol and White House, which was Derek's description of the Naval Academy, as prelude to a piece of Derek's personal business. I did not have to come unless I wanted to, he said, but he would not have it said of himself that he

190

had been to Annapolis, with its National Cemetery, and not been a visitor to the grave of that sailor-patriot, John Paul Jones.

"The *Alfred*," I would say when he paused expectantly, "December 3, 1775." Having provided evidence that I was listening, that I knew my lessons, and that I cared, though I had already decided I didn't care about visiting John Paul Jones's grave, or anybody else's for that matter, I was free to daydream in the sun about our trip while Derek traced our route. In a voice he usually reserved for telling Irish jokes, Derek would very nearly sing the names along our way: Arundel on the Bay, Idlewilde, Herring Bay, Plum Point, the Patuxent River—all preliminary to his favorite, which he always introduced by observing that between Cedar Point and Point Lookout, the northerly and southerly limits on the Chesapeake of St. Mary's County, a peninsula formed by the flow of the Patuxent and Potomac rivers into the bay, there was no point like Point No Point.

"Would you believe now that anyone could name a name like Point No Point? I'm bound to say there's no point to it at all." He was also bound to say it every time, but his joy in the prospect of our journey would have disarmed a far less tolerant audience than the one I provided.

Derek's list of remarkable facts gleaned from the map was not limited to the single entry of Point No Point. He was baffled, for instance, by his discovery that the Wicomico River flowed into the Potomac across the broad water from George Washington's birthplace, and the Great Wicomico emptied into the Chesapeake just beyond the mouth of the Potomac. What puzzled him was that the Wicomico seemed great in size by comparison to the Great Wicomico, which appeared much smaller to both of us. But if he was baffled by the two Wicomico rivers, he was infuriated by the fact that our journey would take us past Mayo in Maryland's Anne Arundel County and Kilmarnock in Virginia's Lancaster County. The Scots and the Irish be damned, said Derek. None of them had the brains God gave porridge or small potatoes. Who else would be stupid enough to put the old country blight upon soil with such sweet English names? To hear him speak the words, "Mayo" and "Kilmarnock" sounded like scabrous diseases.

County names on both shores of the Chesapeake were as comfortable in Derek's mouth as they were fitting, he said, to his ears. Kent, Dorchester, Worcester, Somerset, and Northampton on the Eastern Shore; Northumberland, Lancaster, Gloucester, and York on the west. As I read them from our map of the area, he would find them for me on an English map and tell me what he knew of the original county and the people who inhabited it. More than a decade later, when I visited England for the first time, I found that I could still rely upon the image of Derek's map imprinted in my memory.

Even at the distance of almost thirty years I feel Derek's loss as I write that we never made any of the side trips we had planned after crossing the Potomac into the coastal waters of Virginia. We had enter-

192

tained ourselves with the idea of sailing up the Great
Wicomico just because it looked to be such a piddling
imposter of a river. With what pleasure we looked
forward to traversing the mouth of the Rappahan-
nock, wonderful name, to make our way to the York
River where we would find Yorktown battlefield,
scene of Cornwallis's surrender. Then the final stage
of our search for the past—south beyond Hampton,
around Old Point Comfort, through Hampton Roads,
and up the James River. We described for each other
what restored Williamsburg would look like as we approached it on foot.

We had planned our journey for the summer of
1946 when I would be sixteen years old because Derek
thought that sixteen was old enough to begin exploring the world. I hadn't the courage to tell him my
parents might not think of it in just the same way. I'd
solve that problem when time demanded a solu-
tion—which it never did, for Derek was dead a year by
my sixteenth summer and I had no heart for the journey myself. Not until late spring of 1948, returning to
Baltimore from my hustler's tour of Miami Beach, left
in downtown Richmond by a ride from the North
Carolina line, nursing six dollars and change with my
thumb, tired of moving slowly north along Route 301,
tired of making conversation to keep tired drivers
awake and tired of explaining that what I carried was a
case for a pool cue and not a case for a gun, I saw a sign
in a store window without seeing it and walked the
length of a block before I realized what I might have
seen. Back in front of the window, balanced by cue case

and suitcase, I read the name of Williamsburg among others on the tour advertised by the placard, and decided at that moment to make the detour for Derek's sake as well as my own. Late that afternoon, still carrying my cases, I walked for the first time down Duke of Gloucester Street.

Walking northerly from the James River with Derek would have been better than hitchhiking in from the west by myself. Having my five-hundred-and-fifty-dollar bankroll intact would have been better than possessing just under six dollars after a cheap lunch that left me queasy all the way to Williamsburg. But Derek and my bankroll were both gone, my cue case contained a poolstick more ornament than instrument, my suitcase was full of dirty clothes and my pockets nearly empty, a warm spring rain of large, separated drops was beginning to spatter my last pair of pants, and I had no place to stay the night. What did it all matter if I could walk down Gloucester Street? I would see enough for both of us before I went home to Baltimore.

In spite of my resolution, the increasing rain altered my plans. I had been walking west on Gloucester Street, fatigue forgotten and wetness ignored, searching for the Governor's Palace, which I wrongly remembered from Derek's map as fronting on the street. When I came to Bruton Parish Church, the rain was much heavier and I was sure I had somehow missed the palace. Finding the church open, I entered to save myself and my cue case from the downpour. I would recover but the case was lightly tanned leather, my

194

most valued possession and already badly spotted by the rain. The church was warm and dark; I was suddenly exhausted as I sat on a bench while water flooded down the window panes above me.

I awakened in darkness, knowing neither where I was nor what had awakened me. Because I had slept in a number of strange places during my time in Miami Beach, I had developed the habit of coming to full consciousness with my eyes closed, keeping my wakefulness hidden from the world until I could place myself in it. For a delighted, expanded moment I thought I was in the Reform temple of my youth awaiting my weekly lesson in the Torah. It was my thirteenth year and Mr. Hatcher, the temple organist, was practicing for Sabbath services. The organ's great voice had awakened me from my slumber; in a moment I would arise from the pew and search out the cantor for my lesson.

It was the strap of the cue case, twisted in my hand and painfully taut across my knuckles, that brought me from the temple in Baltimore to the church in Williamsburg. My neck ached from supporting my head as it lolled in sleep against the back of the bench, my upper teeth had sunk deeply into the inside flesh of my lower lip, my mouth had the rancid aftertaste of the bad food I had eaten for lunch, but the music of the organ that had waked me served also to diminish my hurts and let me gather myself behind my eyes. When I was sure again of who and where I was, and that no one was near me, I opened my eyes to a spring evening in Williamsburg. The organist was playing a pensive, unfamiliar piece as I closed the door behind me and walked out into the mist of warm, light rain that covered the church graveyard and Gloucester Street.

Twenty springs later I would be invited to speak to teachers' groups in Hampton and Newport News, who would honor my request for a hotel reservation in Williamsburg even though I would have to rent a car and drive the round trip half a dozen times during three days of meetings. Then I would retrace my steps down Gloucester Street, twenty years of restoration and rebuilding intervening between the past and my memory of it, to Bruton Parish Church, standing in front of the church again as I had done on that other spring evening, this time neither rain nor sleep to confuse me as I deliberately turned west (having that first time meant to return east upon the street to search for a night's shelter in or near the Capitol which lay at its eastern end) to find the Wren Building on the campus of the College of William and Mary, at the western end of Duke of Gloucester Street, where I had spent my three nights in Williamsburg in the spring of 1948. As I walked toward the campus I put my hands in my jacket pockets. They seemed oddly unemployed without cue case and suitcase to hold tightly in their grasp.

Now, having spent a quarter-century in colleges and universities as student and teacher, having visited several hundred campuses to find them more alike in their common sense of repose than different in their individual natures, I like to remember that the first of those campuses was William and Mary, the second oldest college in the United States, where I found shelter and sleep for three damp spring nights. I had never been on a college campus before when I walked through the gate into the college yard to find the Wren Building at a distance before me, the President's House on my right nearly duplicated by the Brafferton on my left, the yard crossed by students walking singly or in pairs and paying no attention to me whatsoever. How can I explain now that I felt welcome *because* no one noticed me, much less stared at me, that I felt such a pang of misery at Derek's absence that I sat upon my suitcase, my back to a red brick wall, and let the gentle movement of the campus comfort me, and that I determined then to spend the rest of my life in such a place if I could. That night I slept in a nest of my own clothes laid on the floor of a classroom in the Wren Building. It was as sweet a bed and as deep a sleep as I have ever had.

For two mornings I hid my small suitcase in an unused fireplace and carried my cue case with me as I explored the colonial heart of a country that had been in growth two hundred and fifty years before I discovered a school named after a Dutchman and his queen who together ruled England and chartered a college in America. My ancestors were Russian peasants living in a village near Kiev when George Washington, whose first monument illuminated my youth, was chancellor for eleven years. Could it be that the nation to which this school belongs, belongs to me as well? That a father born in a dirt-floored hut in central Europe could have a son possessed of America, asleep upon a floor whose original design may have been shaped by Christopher Wren for a college associated with four of the first ten Presidents of the United States? I clutched the strap of my cue case for security and set out to lay claim to it all.

I had no case and no cue to hold when I returned to Williamsburg twenty-four years later with Martha, Paul, and Lisa. Both cue and case had been sold for what cash they would bring, together with clothes and books, when I could no longer meet my college expenses and volunteered for the military draft. Parting with them had been hard, especially since I was able to realize only a fraction of their worth, but my prospects were as barren as my pockets and I had loans from the school that would take me a decade to repay. The boy who bought them was part of that baffling aristocracy who could not play respectable billiards but who coveted leather cases and ivory-inlaid cues as signs and symbols of their competence. For all his incompetence with a cue, he drove a hard bargain.

We motored to Williamsburg after a week's visit with our family in Baltimore. During the respite of a Christmas season spent in others' care I had prepared myself for this return to Williamsburg by wandering the streets of downtown Baltimore, sometimes with Martha and the children, sometimes with Paul alone, most often by myself as I searched for the context in which I had discovered America so that I might be able to convey the possession of it to my son. Because I knew that Baltimore would recur naturally and insistently in his life, I did not intrude it upon him. When I spoke at the Enoch Pratt Free Library, he was there both to hear a speech about a present book and to share a reminiscence about a past life. But when I climbed the two hundred and twenty-eight steps of the Washington Monument, I did it alone that I might recapture whatever remained of that earlier prelude to Williamsburg.

Late December and early January can be gentle in southern Maryland and northern Virginia. At the top of the monument, looking through four barred doors set in the tower at each cardinal point of the compass, a soft unblown rain intermittently spotting the parapets and obscuring the view, I looked south upon the Peabody Conservatory, where my father as a child had faced into a corner while he identified the notes being struck on the piano behind him, and the Walters Art Gallery, newly expanding toward the west, where I had spent so many hours after flag-raising with Derek and before Knocko's poolroom opened for the day's business. The sun returned as I looked down into the square. Two derelicts came out of the bushes, where they had been sheltering from the rain, to sit on the steps leading from the square into the southern portion of Washington Place, while they passed a wine bottle in a brown paper bag between them. The sun also shone upon and reflected from the waters of Baltimore harbor and a corner of the Pratt Library. Even though I could not see it, I knew that Federal Hill rose just across the water to provide the finest natural vantage point above the harbor as it celebrated, through its name, the day in 1788 that Maryland ratified the Federal Constitution.

Derek and I had worked out the details of our journey to tidewater Virginia while we sat on the benches in the monument's shadow, but we had actually conceived the idea when we climbed Federal Hill above the Patapsco on our return from Fort McHenry. I had been so moved by the old fort, by its effect on my sense of America, that I followed unaware where Derek led as we left the fort and began our walk back to the Pratt Street docks. Not until I saw the river did I realize that we had left Fort Avenue to follow more closely the curving banks of the Patapsco's northwest branch as they formed Baltimore's inner harbor. A street sign told me that we were following the route of Francis Scott Key Highway.

Standing above the harbor, both of us still in the grip of a day that had begun with a boat trip to lie offshore beyond Fort McHenry, that had continued with a three-mile walk to the fort from its landward side, that now found us standing where once a tower observatory had signaled and identified incoming ships to Baltimore merchants, we told each other that our morning boat ride had been but a sampling of a river that stretched many miles for the taking. We would take it, Derek said, by the sainted George and Andrew we would float upon both Patapsco and Chesapeake waters until Jamestown and Williamsburg were within range of our sails.

— From Provincetown to Williamsburg —

Some day I shall come upon Williamsburg by boat.
Until then I will have to be content with Interstate 64
and Virginia 60 that brought us on an early January
morning east from Richmond to the eighteenth-
century village Derek was never to see. Virginia's
spacious, rolling terrain easily accommodates four-
lane, divided expressways that are disfiguring to states
more heavily populated. Light rain and unseasonable
warmth had followed us south, the windshield wipers
of our car giving an insistent beat to the slower, un-
dulating rhythm of the roadway. Few cars moved in
either direction, their absence accenting the unpopu-
lated landscape through which we passed. Four of us
apparently well content, three at ease in the pleasure
of anticipation while the fourth gathered memories
with which to clothe brick and wood at a distance
recalled.

"Will it be like Greenfield Village?" We all enjoyed
old Henry Ford's properties even if we didn't like old
Henry Ford.

"Not very much. Greenfield Village is just a collection of buildings in Dearborn brought there from various places, but Williamsburg is still all together the
way it was two hundred years ago. It lets you know how
people really lived then."

"Does it have a museum like Ford Museum?"

"Sure. With cars and locomotives and airplanes
from the eighteenth century. You wouldn't believe
how advanced those early Americans were."

"I'm sorry I asked a dumb question but you don't

have to be nasty. You could just say it was a dumb question."

"All right. It was a dumb question and I'm sorry I was nasty."

I hadn't meant to be sharp or unpleasant. The explosive pace of scientific progress is as unclear to most children as it is to some adults. What would it have cost me to explain the differences between the Ford and Rockefeller collections? As I saw Paul's eyes slide away from mine in the rear-view mirror and felt Martha's irritation in her movement on the seat beside me, I realized that I was nervous and edgy because I was apprehensive about the experience before us. I wanted them to value Williamsburg, to enjoy it as I had, to find it as rich and meaningful as it had been to Derek and to me. But I had seen a black man on a donkey, east of Richmond, riding slowly in the rain with an old piece of blanket held tightly over his head. One hand clasped the blanket beneath his chin while the other held slackly to the rope that served as halter and rein. He was, I knew, a bad omen for our visit.

Paul had used *The Naked Children* as place and reason to begin the conversation. After it was done, I understood that the question had troubled him for a year or more but that we had made it impossible for him to ask and still respect himself. Months after he had managed to ask it, only a few weeks before our journey to Williamsburg, I realized that I had been the primary barrier to the truth he needed to hear: *The Naked Children*, a book about six black children who had been

— From Provincetown to Williamsburg —

my friends in Washington, D. C., had been published in September, and Paul had read it soon thereafter. His opening question, asked at the dinner table, was a flat statement with the question implied.

"There's no kids in my school like the kids in your book. I don't like the black kids in my school. They always try to make trouble."

"You know them all?"

"There's not so many. I know all the ones in the fifth and sixth grades."

"And they'll all troublemakers?"

"Almost every one."

I was just fencing for time, but I should have been prepared. I had known for six months that I would have to deal with the subject. Maybe I should have known for six years, but he had spent four of them in University Elementary School before it had been closed and had begun to attend the neighborhood public school only last year in the fifth grade. University School had been full of children gentled by the unequaled privilege of attention, where hope transforms all but the worst defeats. Far different, in that respect as well as many others, were some of the children from the neighborhood black ghetto who attended nearby elementary and junior high schools. They knew a great deal about the differences between being black and being white, and little of what they knew could have diminished their anger or given them cause to hope. Being troublesome was their real response to the troubled reality of their existence.

Paul had first revealed his feelings to me during a

203

spring evening when I told the story of my afternoon encounter with a group of neighborhood children. I had been returning from a wearying cross-country journey of several days, traffic was heavy, fast, and dangerous for the entire twenty-five miles between our home and the airport, and I was exhausted by the time I reached Ann Arbor. Two blocks from our house I caught up with several groups of students on their way home from the neighborhood junior high school. One group, two boys and three girls, was walking shoulder-to-shoulder in the street, blocking my passage through it. I used my horn gently, thinking they hadn't seen me, to tell them to move toward the curb so that I might pass. What I got in response was the finger from the bigger boy who was walking in the middle, the group continuing to saunter down the street without so much as another backward glance. Wrong place, wrong time, wrong gesture. I hit the brakes so hard the tires squealed, even though I was moving at minimum speed.

The car was still rocking on its springs as I leaped out of the driver's seat and ran past its front end. The smaller boy and girl on the curb side had bolted into the grass verge as I left my car, but the bigger boy held his ground while the two girls on his other side moved from the center of the street to stand behind him.

"Go on! Put that finger up again and I'll break it off!"

"Listen, mister . . ."

"Get your ass off the street before I kick it off!"

They got off the street, I got back in my car, and that

evening when I told the story I was still upset at that boy's stupidity and my anger. But if it was my story, why was Paul's face as flushed when he listened as mine had been when it happened?

"Who were they? Did you know the big boy?" He could barely wait for me to finish my story so that he could ask his question.

"I've seen him around the neighborhood but I don't know his name. He goes to Tappan and I think he lives down on Woodlawn."

"I thought so."

"What did you think?" I suddenly knew what he thought and didn't want to hear him say it.

"I know him. He's a dumb bully."

"Does he bother you?"

"No. I'm too big. He comes over to our school to meet his brother and they pick on little kids."

"How can you be so sure it's the same boy? A lot of kids live down on Woodlawn."

"Was he skinny and black with a big Afro?"

"He was skinny and white with long brown hair."

"But I thought you said he lived down on Wood-lawn."

"I did. But I didn't say he lived on the other side of Packard and I didn't say he was black."

"Maybe you didn't. But that's what those black kids do, so I thought he was black."

"White kids do it too. One of them did it to me." We stared at each other across the table. His face was still flushed. Did mine register the surprise and consternation I felt?

— From Provincetown to Williamsburg —

An eleven-year-old child deserves more opportunity to confront his feelings about human difference than we had given Paul. Racial and religious prejudice had been as reliable as racial and religious ignorance in the families and communities which had raised his mother and me. Because we both learned to disavow that prejudice and to despise that ignorance, even as our families and communities experienced parallel if less powerful change, we have become as intolerant of past attitudes as converts to any new persuasion. Unlike the wrong-headed man who was our country's President twenty years ago, we believed that morality could be legislated, and we have lived long enough to see our belief proven right. What we did not know was that passionate beliefs, pursued to the end of dramatic change, can be as corrupting to the pursuer as absolute power to the powerful. Our private and professional pursuit, begun a decade before Paul's birth, intensified during the years of his life with us, had left no room in our family for the fair observation of difference. I would have flatly denied such an accusation until the moment my son enacted its truth before my eyes.

"Have you been having trouble with black kids?"

"Everybody does. They're a bunch of rats." No tentativeness, no apology—it was I who looked away as he spoke. Too much of what he said had obviously been accumulated and repressed for the past year, building up pressure inside the child because it could find no room for expansion within our household. In our anxious expurgation of prejudice and ignorance, we had also purged the portion of reality that protects against the acts of the furious while understanding the cause of their fury. An exasperated eleven-year-old boy, not in the least disturbed or deterred by mistaking a white with long brown hair for a black with an Afro, taught me a detailed and painful lesson in the visitation of the sins of the fathers upon the children. When he had done, we had only begun, for then it was my turn; my portion was explanation and apology.

I had never been to public school with blacks, I told him, because Baltimore had been a Jim Crow town until the court decisions of the fifties began to legislate morality. I had returned to my high school in 1957, a decade after graduation, to be told by the principal that boys coming from black junior high schools had been three to four years behind their white counterparts when schools had been integrated in 1954. Only now, he said, after three years of intense effort and almost continuous misunderstanding, did it seem possible to deal with such different levels of attainment together in the same classrooms. For the first year, at least, he had despaired of educating the whites at all because the blacks were so much more in need. In the long run he thought the terrible inequities would be righted. But he could find no peace for himself in the realization of what had been allowed to pass for education of black children during his many years in the school system.

"But that was then. Now is different. People don't do

dumb things like they used to. Everybody goes to the same schools and gets the same education. Everything's different."

"Don't you believe it. Only some things are different. You and black kids may go to the same school but you don't get the same education. Not by a long shot!"

"We do too!" He was indignant that I could be so wrong, that I didn't know how school really was. His indignation subsided as we talked about the different educations available in the same school to children whose parents know how to make use of the system and to those whose parents do not. To children, like himself, whose parents use books—still the currency of the schools—as one of their primary means to understand the world, by contrast to children whose parents may find written language alien and uncomfortable.

"A lot of black kids talk funny."

"You mean they don't talk like you."

"Well, they don't talk like you either."

"But you talk like me and so do all your teachers. And we all talk like most of the people who speak on television or on the radio. How do you think those black kids feel when they find out that what their families and friends say, which is also what they say, is no good in the ears of their teachers? How angry would you be if people tried to teach you that your mother and father's way of speaking is no good, which is the same as teaching you to be ashamed of them and, worst of all, to be ashamed of yourself?"

We talked about the position that American blacks found themselves in a hundred years after the Civil

208

—From Provincetown to Williamsburg —

War released them from overt slavery. How they no longer belong, like horses or dogs, to someone else, but how they aren't their own property in the same way that he and I belong to ourselves. What does it mean to be *self-possessed*? We agreed that it means to be enough in control of your own life so that you don't have to ask permission to exist and you don't have to search for yourself by looking in other people's eyes.

"The black kids in my school—they're different from the black kids who were in University School."

"And you're different from most of the white kids in my poolroom. You know something they never knew—you know you're going to make it. Your biggest problem is to identify *how*, which is pretty much the same problem that black kids had in University School. They knew they were on top and they expected to stay there. That's what made them so different from the black kids in your school now. They didn't have the same reasons to feel frustrated or angry, so they weren't."

"Do people still have slaves?"

"Not in this country, though I've been in some parts of the South where blacks still live like slaves and whites treat blacks like they still owned them."

"I hate having slaves and I hate the South!"

I reminded him that my mother, his grandmother, was born and bred in the South, that she had grown up with the hateful word "nigger" in her ears and in her mouth, but that she had come a long way from that kind of ignorant prejudice in the seventy years of her life, and so had the South. Further maybe than the

—From Provincetown to Williamsburg —

North, I told him. You only have to spend a little time with schoolchildren in some parts of Harlem to know that no one, black or red or white, has worse living conditions anywhere in the United States. But you don't have to go as far as Harlem, I said. Parts of Detroit would do just as well.

We said much more to each other about black and white in America, but all I could remember clearly when I saw the black man on the donkey east of Richmond, a piece of blanket held over his head against the rain, was Paul's passionate denunciation of slavery and the South. I had all but memorized the official guidebook to colonial Williamsburg, which contains the briefest possible truth about the slavery of the period: "Some of the pleasures but few of the promises of this life extended to black Virginians . . . in town or country [the black] was regarded first as property and only incidentally as a person. . . . In Williamsburg, an 'urban center' of its time, about half the population was Negro. Five out of six local families owned one or more slaves, and scores more were required for work at inns and taverns." If the words were passive, the truth they reproduced was not. Paul would have the opportunity to see the "most historic avenue in America" at its best and worst. As we drove slowly along Francis Street toward out lodging in the Williamsburg Inn, we passed a carriage full of white adults and children taking advantage of the mild weather to enjoy contemporary transportation through the streets of the town. Their color was right even if their clothes were wrong. But the eighteenth-century car-

210

riage and costumed driver were both entirely authentic. Both were black.

The cost of our connecting rooms in the inn had been the subject of discussion when I called from Baltimore for reservations. Paul had heard me say to the young woman who quoted the price that I only wanted to rent the rooms for several nights. I didn't want to buy them. She had laughed and agreed that the prices were terrible; when her family came to visit, she said, they stayed in the motor lodge, which was nice enough and right next to the inn. Would I like her to transfer my call to the lodge? I thanked her for her kindness and declined. Though overpriced, the period appointments of the inn make it a unique base for a visit to Williamsburg. To balance my inexplicable feelings of discomfort and uncertainty about our visit, I wanted our search for the past to enjoy every possible advantage of the present.

Remembering my telephone conversation, Paul's first comment upon our rooms was that they were "awful small for such a richey place." They were, I allowed, somewhat smaller than the average motel might provide at half the price, but they were also furnished with attention to detail found in only a few hostelries anywhere in the world. The furnishings were such fine reproductions that only a little effort was required to imagine yourself as a guest in an eighteenth-century Williamsburg home. Yes, said my son to my back as I hung up my clothes, just a little effort and a lot of money. That's all you needed to be a guest in a Williamsburg home. No, I thought, my back

211

still turned, all you needed two centuries ago was effort, money, and a white skin. The black man on the
donkey and the black man driving the carriage were
too much on my mind.

The long afternoon was rich and pleasant for all of
us, but particularly sweet for me. Nothing was por-
tentous, nothing ominous, and I was able to watch my
family enjoy Williamsburg—I admit I had come to
think of it as *my* Williamsburg, even as I think of it as *my*
country—not only in ways I had planned and anticipated, but in ways that even great optimism could
hardly have expected. At the Information Center,
where we began our visit with the thirty-five-minute
film, *Williamsburg—The Story of a Patriot*, a film I had
never seen whose innocence swept away my critical
faculties and left me deeply moved (a middle-aged
American remembering a bandy-legged little Englishman who would gladly have walked from Baltimore to Williamsburg to see such a film), we were told
by an attendant that we had picked the one week in the
past year when the town did not seem to be overrun
with visitors. Sometimes you can't get the feel of the
village for all the bodies, she said. It's on days like this
my husband and I like to go walking through the
streets in the early evening. You can almost imagine it's
1772 instead of 1972, especially with people afraid of a
little rain and keeping indoors.

It was the rain that gave a remembered perfection to
our visit. How like that other time it was, warm and
gentle, obscuring faces and erasing evidence of modern intrusion into a more elemental world. If our

jackets, hats, and umbrellas were unfitting, at least for us they were unobtrusive and we were able to walk the late afternoon streets in the solitude created by weather and season. Delighted with the feeling that the empty village was theirs, Paul and Lisa led us from shop to shop where we four and the shopkeeper were often the only occupants.

Our first shop was our most fortunate. The man playing the role of apothecary must have been feeling the weight of the darkening afternoon, for his welcome to us was as warm and genuine as it may have been practiced, and he volunteered detailed, entertaining answers almost before we could formulate our questions. Not only was he an apothecary, he told us, but he was also a doctor "very good too at removing a bothersome limb." Paul's eyes were round with fascination and mild horror as our friendly apothecary and surgeon, alternating between the roles of the two men who had once been in partnership in the shop, graphically demonstrated the uses of his "compleat sett of amputating instruments." A sensitive man as well as a fine actor, he concluded his performance by sending us down the street to the kitchen bakery of the Raleigh Tavern where he just happened to know, he told the children, that fresh gingerbread cookies were at that moment coming out of the red brick ovens.

If the apothecary shop had been an ideal beginning point for the children, the Raleigh Tavern could not have been better suited for me. After buying a bag full of cookies in the separate kitchen, we decided to tour the tavern even though the children were anxious to go on to more shops. Upon entering at the front door we were ushered into the game room to await the woman who would conduct us through the building. Last into the room, I was too busy reading the guidebook I carried to look about me immediately. When I raised my eyes to find a seat in the familiar room, I suddenly felt myself the victim of a cosmic joke. My hand involuntarily tightened about the strap of the cue case long since sold but once carried into this same room almost a quarter century before. Then it had contained chairs and tables, as it had only two years before when I had briefly rediscovered the village. Now it was nearly empty except for a single object, but with that single object it was nearly full. Borne up on row after imposing row of graceful legs; six feet wide by twelve feet long, seventy-two square feet of taut green cloth; there before me was the biggest pocket billiard table my eyes had ever seen. I stared at it like a man without a cue until my family led me away to a nearby bench. Seated upon the bench I momentarily closed my eyes, expecting when I opened them to awaken in Bruton Parish Church, strap of the cue case biting into my knuckles as rain ran down the window panes above my head.

But it was still the Raleigh Tavern when I opened my eyes to the sound of the door being closed by the beautifully costumed woman who was to be our guide, and it was still the tavern some twenty-five minutes later when we had completed our tour of the building that housed the first meeting of charter members of the Phi Beta Kappa Society, of the five patriots who led

214

— From Provincetown to Williamsburg —

the founding of Virginia's Committee of Correspondence, of the Assembly representatives who issued the first call for the Continental Congress, and of the Williamsburg Volunteers who drank to Peyton Randolph newly returned from Philadelphia where he had served as first president of that Congress. Patrick Henry's troops gave their leader a dinner in the same great room, the Apollo, which saw the citizens of Williamsburg celebrate the signing of the Treaty of Paris that brought an end to the Revolutionary War. The Apollo was also the room in which Thomas Jefferson, a dozen years before that celebration, had danced away the night with the lovely Belinda and awakened the next morning with an ugly hangover.

Whoever they were, whatever their status, if they slept at the tavern they slept on a straw-filled mattress supported upon a platform of ropes. Having once slept on just such a pallet, I know how much better bedded I was at the Wren Building in a nest of my own clothes placed upon the floor. Until Providence put that billiard table in my way, memories of my earliest visit had been retreating before the insistent reality of the children's presence. As we finished our tour and they walked outside to look with new eyes at the area in front of the tavern where, we were told, slaves had regularly been bought and sold, I searched out the person in charge of the building to offer him a piece of information that would give the exhibition in the Raleigh greater authenticity and give me the small reward I longed to claim. I was acutely conscious of wanting to leave something of myself behind.

Leaving his mother and sister outside the building,
Paul joined me as I crossed the front hall of the tavern
to search for a custodian in the office behind the stairs.
One of the costumed young men in the room, part of a
small group taking their ease on a quiet day, said that
he would be glad to speak for me to the curator who
was not then available. About the billiard table? Yes, it
was a real prize, possessing even its original cloth when
first put on exhibition, which was only recently, but
re-covered now because the cloth had begun to wear
badly as a result of being rubbed by too many curious
hands. And it certainly was the biggest pocket billiard
table any of them had ever seen. He himself was a pool
player and had never seen anything like it. Did I have
some information about it that I wanted him to convey
to the curator?

It would be easy to explain what I had in mind to
another pool player like himself, I said, because he
would know the difference between table requirements of pocket billiard games on the one hand and
straight-rail or three-cushion billiards on the other.

"You mean that one table has pockets and the
other doesn't?" he said, looking slightly mystified.

"Right. And the game with three balls, two white and
one red, is played on the table without pockets?"

"Yes."

"But this table has the usual six pockets and it's all set
up for a billiards game. You can't play pool with those
three balls on the table. You can only play some form
of billiards."

216

— From Provincetown to Williamsburg —

He was amazed and embarrassed that he had worked there for months and never seen it. And think of all the people who had passed it by and never noticed or said a word. Yes, I thought, as he showed us to the door with thanks and a promise to see that the exhibition was put right, but perhaps none of them carried a cue case through the village on his first visit or wanted so much to give something in return for the gift of the past that Williamsburg gives of itself.

"That was good. You really knew." Paul patted me on the arm as we walked out the door to the place where slaves once were bought and sold. His face and tone reflected his pride. Even if I was a nothing-and-six fighter, I still knew a lot about pool.

Though the time was mid-afternoon, the day was so soon after the shortest day of the year that light was beginning to lessen all about us. With impending darkness and a thickening of the mild mist again into rain, Duke of Gloucester Street belonged solely to us. The feeling of isolation, of suspension in space and time without the sustaining presence of others, was so strong that the children reached for our hands as we reached for them and for each other. Standing within that marketplace for slaves, itself part of a living monument to freedom, the sharp edge of both realities dulled by the soft gray rain, we felt the weight of the past and huddled together for comfort and reassurance. As we stood silently, saying nothing, each under the influence of the past in muted life, a door opened in a house farther along the street and the figure of a large man intruded itself upon our reverie.

Hooded against the light rain, the man came toward us on the brick sidewalk across the street. As he came closer I knew his garment to be the long cloak worn by Williamsburg employees costumed in keeping with the era of the buildings that surrounded us. Because nothing else moved within range of my vision, my eyes incuriously followed the man as he walked with heavy, unhurried gait until he came opposite us and then crossed the street toward the tavern corner behind us.

"Good evening." I had spoken first as I recognized the broad, pleasant face of the baker who had sold us cookies from the Raleigh Tavern kitchen within the past hour.

"Evening, suh." He smiled as he recognized us, then turned the tavern corner and passed from our sight in the direction of his bakery.

"Daddy?" Holding his sister's hand and the diminished bag of cookies, Paul was staring at the spot where the man had disappeared from view.

"Yes?"

"Did Noel have slaves in his family?" The resemblance was striking, yet neither of us had remarked it an hour earlier in the bakery. Was it this place where we stood, combined with the hooded cloak which obscured the visual difference between Noel's Afro and this man's close-cropped hair?

"Noel's grandparents on his mother's side were both born slaves and so was his grandmother on his father's side. His father's father was a white man."

"Did white men marry slaves?"

218

"His grandmother wasn't a slave by the time his grandfather got her pregnant. And they weren't married. White men didn't marry black women in those days. They just used them up, one way or another."

"Ant then sold them at places like this."

"Yes. They did that too."

Paul grimaced with anger and disgust, but the words he was about to speak never left his mouth. At that moment, carrying a large sack, the baker reappeared around the corner of the tavern and passed within a few yards of us as he again crossed the street to the opposite sidewalk. We acknowledged each other this time with a nod as I looked as long as I might without staring at the broad planes and generous features of his face. From some angles he looked remarkably like Noel. For a moment I thought of asking him if he were related to the Bookman family, but the thought came to nothing as he left us behind on the street.

"Would Noel like it here?" Paul's mind was pursuing the same train of thought. I was surprised to find how reluctant I was to think or to talk about Noel and Williamsburg. I would have been happier had the man looked like someone else.

"I don't know. You can ask him when we get back." I was ashamed of my answer even as I made it. Noel and I had come to know each other through our work in a prison school in southeastern Michigan. Because we had worked out some difficult problems together, and those problems often required almost immediate solutions, Noel had spent a good deal of time at our house as the most convenient meeting place for discussions and arguments that sometimes wore out the night. As the first black adult whom Paul had known, to whom he had listened as we spoke about prison problems which were frequently measured in dimensions of black and white, Noel spoke for a segment of the adult world that was otherwise voiceless in Paul's experience. He deserved a much better answer to his probing question than I had given him.

"Look. It's a hard question. I didn't mean to turn you off. I just don't know what the answer is. Do you think he'd like it here?"

"No. I don't know. Maybe."

"That's about three different answers."

"Well, it's hard. Everything's nice except when they tell you about where they used to buy and sell black people. I hate that and so would Noel. He'd hate it worse than I do."

"No doubt about it. But maybe he wouldn't let it stand in his way. This country, bad and good, is as much his as it is yours and mine. Maybe more. His family's been here a lot longer than mine and suffered a lot more to get what it's got. If I think about Williamsburg as mine, how about Noel? His family could have been living *right here* two hundred years ago. This street we're on could belong to him and his kids in a way that it could never belong to us."

"I guess so." Nothing sounds so unconvinced as a child who's been told he should feel one thing when he feels another. As Paul's eyes slipped away from mine, I knew I'd have to do better. Given a fair chance, perhaps Williamsburg would help me.

—From Provincetown to Williamsburg—

In the next three hours we gave Williamsburg every chance and it, in turn, gave a prime performance. From the Raleigh we crossed the street, in the tracks of the baker who looked like Noel, to visit the wig-maker—the barbershop of the eighteenth century, this one serving Thomas Jefferson and Patrick Henry, among many others—and to reject poor Wetherburn's Tavern when the children complained that they had already seen one tavern and that was enough, then recrossed the quiet street to watch a jeweler, a clock-maker, and an engraver pursue their crafts under the Sign of the Golden Ball. Next was the milliner's shop for the latest London fashions in hats, where we dis-covered that a cardinal may be a bird but it is also a short, hooded scarlet cloak; then diagonally across the intersection of Botecourt and Gloucester streets to the home of the music teacher, passing on the way the first person we had seen on the street since our encounter with the baker. She too was an employee of Williams-burg, a gowned and cloaked hostess wearing a magni-ficent scarlet cardinal. Encountering her immediately after the milliner's shop, we felt as if she had been directed to stroll on Gloucester Street at just that mo-ment solely for our benefit. Though no one else was there to see her, we were as appreciative an audience as anyone could want.

The music teacher was as cordial in his welcome as the apothecary had been, and equally pleased to play his role by playing his instruments for us. While we warmed ourselves before his comfortable fire, the dampness of the day rising from us as the welcome heat dried our clothes, he took up his fiddle and played small but stately dances that filled the room with their careful patterns of sound. Alone, I would have stayed the afternoon, turning myself in the heat of the fire while watching his competent hands re-create an age, his face as intent when he fiddled as Paul's or the boy who played Tchaikovsky and Tele-mann on Fifty-third Street in New York. But the children were soon refreshed, and the day was already far upon the wane. Ruffles at his wrists and throat, fiddle in one hand and bow in the other, knee breeches and buckled shoes, our host bade us farewell in his doorway, the fire behind him laying flickering shadows where recently we had stood.

As we walked west again upon Duke of Gloucester Street, the music master's fire-wrought shadows seemed to follow behind us. Above the college at the far end of the street we could see the lowering sun for the first time in two days, rain still in the air about us but the western sky clearing for sunset. We turned to see our shadows lengthen along the street toward the Capitol at its eastern end, turning in time to see our recent host raise his bow in greeting to a pair of women in cardinals who were a show in scarlet as they entered the Brick House Tavern. The scene could only have been arranged for us by that same manager who had also provided the light rain to discourage other vis-itors, the warm welcome from apothecary and music master, and the various joys of the Raleigh. The air about us glistened as we made our way beyond the post office to the printer's and bookbinder's, home of the first newspaper in Virginia.

Printer, bookbinder, Prentis's Store; then past Chowning's Tavern to stop for a moment in the old courthouse of 1770, now a museum but soon to be internally restored to recall its judicial functions of almost two centuries; across the street to bootmaker, spinner and weaver, and cooper who locked his door after us, for we had been his last visitors of the day. Even the insatiable children were slow and satisfied as we straggled once more across our historic avenue to read the headstones in Bruton Parish churchyard.

Experienced in the ways of old burial places, Martha and Paul went off by themselves to look for famous names and colonial dates. Left to ourselves, holding hands against the falling light, Lisa and I wandered aimlessly among gravestones, saying nothing, each occupied with the last of our gingerbread cookies as well as the nameless, quiet thoughts that may come in a churchyard at the end of so sweet an afternoon. Slowly we made our way around the perimeter wall until we found ourselves back at the west entrance to the church, the one that led through the base of the tower into the foot of the nave, the one which still held the bench I had slept upon, rain upon the window and cue case held tightly in hand, almost a quarter of a century before. I turned once to search for Martha and Paul, saw them distantly in a corner of the yard, and realized that I did not want to impose the past upon them. For them, Bruton Parish Church would be an interesting example of colonial American architecture, an unremarkable bench and pleasant organ evocative of a story once told by their husband and father. Like Fort McHenry, Bruton Church was more for keeping than giving. Lisa was the perfect companion, walking with me slowly through tower and nave to the chancel where we stood quietly for a few moments as I remembered the organ played pensively years before. We turned then and retraced our steps to the west door where Martha and Paul awaited us. Tired now, not talking, all four of us were ready to make our way back to our lodgings.

By unspoken agreement we dined early that night. The first family seated in the beautifully appointed dining room of the inn, we had its facilities almost to ourselves for an hour. Having only one other diner at his tables, our waiter attended us superbly, anticipating the tired children in their needs as well as their oversights. His deft, friendly service and easy conversation with all of us, but especially with the children, drew us into conversation with each other that otherwise the weight of a long day might have repressed.

"That baker. He really looked like Noel." Paul's eyelids looked as heavy as mine felt, but his mind was still ranging over the day.

"It was the set of his eyes, so wide apart, and the shape of his face. His skin color, too. Sort of red and tan, like Noel." I, too, had thought about him and decided that the man's skin color was the essential element in the resemblance. It had been so near a duplicate of Noel's unusual coloring that I could visualize it hours after seeing him on the street. As I sat at the table and remembered the day, I realized why I had been so sure of Noel's reaction to Williamsburg.

"Do you remember when Noel and Florida moved to Ann Arbor from Dexter?" Paul smiled broadly at Flo's full name. When I had told him about making the mistake of calling her Florence, discovering thereby that Flo could stand for Florida as well, he had been delighted with the name and pleased at its every mention.

"Sure. I liked that big old house they lived in out there."

"So did they, except in winter when they thought they'd freeze to death. Anyway, that's why they moved. Do you remember what happened after they moved into their apartment over on the other side of the stadium?"

"Somebody did something mean to them?"

Though we had talked about it a great deal at the time, almost three years before our visit to Williamsburg, he had been too young to understand much of what had happened and we had not pressed it hard upon him. I reminded him that the "something mean" had been produced by a particularly ugly case of racial sickness. Having more time than Noel to look for an apartment, Flo had found one that seemed suited to them in size, price, and location. She herself had completed all the necessary arrangements and they had moved in on the day after Labor Day. In quick succession, within the next week, rotten eggs and tomatoes were spattered on their front windows when they were

225

both at work, a white cross was painted on their front door, they received phone calls threatening to bomb their cars unless they moved out, and finally a large wooden cross was set afire on the lawn in front of their building. What made the whole thing unreal, Noel told me, was that at least three other black couples inhabited various parts of the large apartment complex, and they had never had even a suggestion of trouble.

After the cross-burning, which had done considerable damage to grass and shrubbery, the apartment manager called upon them to suggest that maybe the best thing was just to move out before somebody got hurt. Noel, who had spent his adolescence in street gangs in Detroit, told him he wasn't moving anywhere. Instead, he was organizing his friends from the prison to do spot guard duty on his apartment on an irregular but around-the-clock schedule, so that no one could know when it was being watched and when it wasn't, and every one of his friends would be legally armed and ready to shoot any son of a bitch who came looking for trouble. This, he said to the manager, who had a soft but decided southern accent, was one pair of niggers who wasn't going to run.

"*Pair* of niggers . . . !" said the southerner, the phrase escaping him before he could shut his mouth, his eyes wide in obvious amazement. From that moment, said Noel, he realized that their troubles were over. Theirs, but not the manager's. After waiting a week to be sure, Noel had slashed the tires on the manager's car, all four of them, and poured a pound of sugar in his gas tank. For a month he'd had his

226

friends on night duty at the prison make phone calls to the manager every hour on the hour from midnight through six o'clock. When the manager had taken his receiver off the hook, Noel had gotten friends using names of residents in the apartment complex to call the management company and complain loudly and repeatedly that the manager was unreachable by phone between midnight and six A.M., no matter what the emergency. When his phone went back on the hook, the calls had resumed, this time at half-hour intervals. Four more slashed tires combined with another pound of sugar, and the manager had moved out. Since the day of the interview in their apartment, Noel had never spoken another word to him.

"But why did he do all that? What did the manager do to him?" Paul was flabbergasted, but no more than I had been when Noel ʜad told me the same story, searching for the same effect and obtaining it when I told him I thought he was out of his mind. Just because the man had repeated his phrase, "pair of niggers."

"You're right about one thing anyway," Noel said, with a smile and an accent that were as offensive as he meant them to be. "Whitey, he don't know nothing 'bout being no nigger."

And then he told me what every black man who knew Florida and himself would have *known* when he saw that manager's face and heard his words. Though he had waited a week to be sure, he had known that the man was responsible for their troubles as soon as he heard the tone and emphasis of his *"pair* of niggers." Florida was so light-colored that she could have chosen

227

to cross over. Instead she had chosen to marry him, with his odd black and red and tan coloring and especially with his Afro which he had been earliest among their friends to grow. That hillbilly trash had met Florida first, had taken her for white, then had seen him and thought she was a white woman living with a black man. Maybe he was conditioned to black couples in the apartment building because they were already there when he took the job. But he didn't have to put up with a black man living with a white woman, so he'd called out the Klan. He'd got what was coming to him.

Paul was as silent as I had been when Noel told me the story. Did it have the same meaning for him that it did for me? I told him what I thought: "I don't think Noel would run from slavery in Williamsburg if he wouldn't run from the Klan in Ann Arbor."

"Well, I never thought he'd run away either."

"I said *run* but that's not exactly what I meant. I was trying to say that I think he'd enjoy Williamsburg the way we do and he wouldn't be put off by reminders of slavery because he's already got a place inside himself for things like that."

"He wouldn't like it."

"No, but he wouldn't let it keep him from the good things a place like this has to offer." Three of us were aware that the real moral of my story had little to do with Noel and much to do with us. As we left the dining room, nearly somnambulant from the combined effects of good food, a warm room, and the day's great length, thinking of Noel, the baker, and the slave market in front of the Raleigh Tavern, I could not help

228

noticing that the line of guests now waiting to be seated was as white as the staff of the dining room was black. Would Noel care more about that than he would about slavery in the eighteenth century? Paul could ask him if Paul wanted to know. I was tired of hard questions, mine as well as his. Nothing was as simple as once I had thought.

Looked at searchingly the next day, until courtesy forced us to drop our eyes, to glance away and pretend an interest in something else, the baker at the Raleigh did not look so much like Noel after all. But nothing looked quite the same in the sunshine of our second day in Williamsburg as it had looked in the rain and mist of the first. We had been fortunate in our itinerary because we had seen the shops and taverns in the unfocused light that gives Duke of Gloucester Street its greatest reality. Upon Capitol and Governor's Palace, however, the quality of light can have little effect. Both seem immutable, as changeless in weather and season as they are in time, impossible that both should be reconstructions of buildings gutted and leveled by fire in the same century in which they were built. In part because of the sense of permanence that each conveys, both are monumental, not only uninhabited but essentially uninhabitable, demanding only the resident care of attendants and the transient attention of visitors. Between visits to the Capitol and palace, immensely impressed but equally unengaged, we stopped again at the Raleigh kitchen to buy gingerbread cookies and to refresh our sense of human scale.

"You folks get a little bit wet on yesterday?" The

229

— From Provincetown to Williamsburg —

baker had needed a moment to recognize us without our rain gear.

"A little, but I liked it when it was raining. Everybody else stayed home." Paul was paying for the cookies, waiting for his change and carrying our part of the conversation.

"Yep. Winter rain here makes for good seeing if you don't mind being wet on. Coming from the Capitol?"

"And on our way to the palace," I said. Paul was too busy counting his change to reply immediately. "Anything you specially recommend for us to see?"

"Nice day like this, middle of the morning they might be a few people all dressed up and standing round on the corner just looking natural. They sure do make it look like it ain't today."

"Much obliged. And you have a nice day, hear?"

As we walked out of the kitchen door into the tavern garden, Paul elbowed me in the ribs and spoke in a harsh whisper: "That was nasty! Why did you make fun of him?"

"Make fun of him?" I was indignant at his undeserved criticism and angry at his sharp elbow. He was getting too big and too strong to use me like that. "I never did! Why did you say that?"

"And you have a nice day, hear?" Paul mimicked me, his face flushed, his voice capturing perfectly my own laid-on southern idiom and mild accent. "You don't talk like that! You were making fun of him."

"Do you really think I'd do that?"

"No, but you did. I heard you."

230

—From Provincetown to Williamsburg—

"I wasn't speaking for your ears. I was speaking for his."

"What does that mean? You can't talk me out of it. I *heard* you!"

As hard to explain to my son as it is to myself when it happens is the practice of adapting more than words to person and place. I have spoken with others who do it. For some it is unconscious, they say, while some are aware of it but not as a matter of choice. I have done it twice more in Paul's hearing, once with a Scots/Canadian at Niagara Falls and again with a New York taxi driver. Both incidents brought the same intolerant reaction from him and the same angry denial from me. But only the occurrence at Williamsburg was a prelude to Paul's rejection of a part of his own inheritance.

We were both angry as we walked west on Gloucester Street toward the point where it is crossed by the palace green, the palace itself rising two blocks to the north. I persisted in trying to explain and explain away something that was both inexplicable and offensive to him, as he made clear to me when we paused to wait for Martha and Lisa to catch up with our angry pace. We were both so absorbed in our difference that neither of us noticed we were not being overtaken by our companions even though we had stopped at an intersection to wait for them. It was Paul, having less invested in the argument than I, who saw the small but growing crowd of spectators on a corner we had passed and turned us back toward them. We were both still warm

231

from our heated discussion when we joined Martha and Lisa on the edge of the group.

"Look at her hands," Martha turned to me and whispered as we came up behind them. "Don't they look just like Queen Elizabeth's in that painting we saw in the Capitol?"

"But she's pretty. That queen was ugly." Paul had overheard. Both of them were right. One of the women in the tableau on the corner before us—the baker's group of people all dressed up and just standing around looking natural—had exquisite hands which she used so expressively, even when they lay at rest upon her escort's arm, that together they formed a separate character in the carefully balanced scene before us. And she was as handsome in her simple eighteenth-century costume as the Virgin Queen had been ugly in her magnificent sixteenth-century gown. I turned to Paul to tell him that I too thought she was a pretty woman, but he was no longer beside me. Looking through the small crowd, I found the back of his head at the front of the spectators. Something about the tableau had drawn him like a magnet to its side.

The actors in our scene, divided into three couples with their attendant blacks, standing in front of the Orlando Jones home on the corner of Gloucester and Colonial streets, had obviously met on market day, for the servants all carried capacious but empty baskets. Beautifully costumed, easily posed, their animated conversation conveyed such reality to our surroundings that I understood what the baker had meant when he said *They sure do make it look like it ain't today.* The crowd was motionless, spellbound with appreciation.

When the couples dispersed, from their conversation apparently to visit several shops before making their separate ways to market (the scene was so convincing that I actually looked on our detailed map of the restored area for the marketplace), each walked slowly off in a different direction, trailed by one or several servants. We followed even more slowly after the couple walking west on Gloucester Street, admiring their costumes and their presence until they left us at Market Square Tavern. Still in the grip of their dramatic reality, I looked once more for nonexistent vendors on the green of the square.

"Those costumes and the way they wear them . . ." Martha too had been affected. The Capitol had been meant for the royal and the great, but the streetcorner scene had been for us.

"I thought the servants were the perfect touch. Just being there, they made the whole scene." I had so much more to say. Just as the introductory film had moved me with its great patriotic innocence, so had the simple surface of the tableau fired my imagination and removed me bodily to its more elemental world. I wanted to talk about it, to say something of Derek and sailing down the Chesapeake toward Jamestown Island, of three nights on the floor of a classroom in the Wren Building, of all that and much more. But in Paul's voice the sharp edge of the present cut through the fabric of the past, and I was left with cloth that was thin and rent.

"You should say what they really were."

"Who?"

"You called them servants. That's not what they were. They were slaves."

"All right. They were slaves, but . . ."

"It's not all right. I hated it. Nobody should ever have to do that."

"Have to do what?"

"Be black now and have to play a slave. That's what's wrong with this whole place. It's full of slaves and . . . and things like that."

He was angry, and confused by my failure to share his anger. I was bewildered by his reaction, and thought myself doubly betrayed when I discovered that Martha felt much as he did, even if she chose a different way to express it. For her, Williamsburg was as admirable in its artfulness as I had found it, and some of it equally moving. But she wondered why the Rockefellers had spent their money to recreate a town built on slavery? Could they not have chosen to reconstruct colonial life in a place where half the population was not always regarded and often treated as something less than human? She is glad we went, she says, but once was enough. Neither she nor Paul has any desire to return to Williamsburg.

I am dismayed, but I will not be discouraged from the attempt to convey a few of my possessions to my son. Knocko's poolroom has shown me the error of delay, the terrible speed with which the past may pass beyond giving, while the disassembled gun that accompanies us each summer from Ann Arbor to Truro is mute evidence of what I have already given.

— From Provincetown to Williamsburg —

Though I have withdrawn Fort McHenry from my list of conveyance, the belief grows upon me that its withdrawal may be temporary. Vietnam recedes. If Fort McHenry passes between us, it will happen because the flag possesses its own vital force. *Maybe I'll sew it back on my jacket because I like it,* he says now, two years after he had intended to debase it. I smile with the pleasure he gives me. And I smile because I know that I will continue to sing "The Star Spangled Banner" badly and he can do as he likes.